STRAIGHT TALK
TALK
with YOUR
KIDS
ABOUT
SEX

Josh & Dottie
McDOWELL

HARVEST HOUSE PUBLISHERS
EUGENE, OREGON

STRAIGHT TALK WITH YOUR KIDS ABOUT SEX

Copyright © 2012 by Josh McDowell Ministry. All rights reserved.
Published by Harvest House Publishers
Eugene, Oregon 97402
www.harvesthousepublishers.com

Library of Congress Cataloging-in-Publication Data

McDowell, Josh.
    Straight talk with your kids about sex / Josh and Dottie McDowell.
    p. cm.
    ISBN 978-0-7369-4992-7 (pbk.)
    ISBN 978-0-7369-4993-4 (eBook)
    1. Sex instruction. 2. Christian ethics. I. McDowell, Dottie. II. Title.
    HQ56.M16 2012
    649'.65Sex education.--dc23
                                                            2012016887

Printed in the United States of America

12 13 14 15 16 17 18 19 20 / BP-GLD / 10 9 8 7 6 5 4 3 2 1

To parents who, with courage and conviction, lovingly share with their children God's purpose for sex—often and openly—throughout the child-rearing process.

CONTENTS

For further research, documentation, and critical insights on each chapter, go to www.josh.org/straighttalk.

Chapter 1

Just One Click Away

Sex. To some people it's a dirty word, to others a beautiful one. And to still others it's a provocative word...something they're not comfortable talking about. Whatever your attitude, sex is a sensitive yet immensely important issue. For those who believe it's a marvelous but powerful force that should not be misused, such as parents or leaders working with youth, the idea of sex—sexual activity— among young people is loaded with plenty of concern.

So how concerned would you be if a stranger was slipping into your child's bedroom every day? What if this intruder was systematically teaching your child a distorted and perverted concept of sex? And what if this "sex education" your child was receiving led them down a path to immoral sex? You would no doubt be frightened and infuriated that the mind and heart of your child was being violated by this menacing intruder.

But before we go on to explain this danger, let us say this. We (Josh and Dottie), as parents who have raised four children of our own, are not here just to alarm you, although you have reason to be alarmed. We also want to equip you with a clear strategy to counter what your kids are facing. Even more at the heart of what we want to do, we hope to supply you with effective tools to raise your kids with a healthy (godly) understanding of sex.

After all, sex is great. It's marvelous. It's so wonderful that it can't be put into words—because God has made it that way. You no doubt want your children to grow up understanding and embracing his design for their sexuality so they can delight in sex as he meant it to be delighted in. And if an immoral intruder were to cause your kids to misuse God's wonderful gift, you would be angry and heartbroken.

Studies have shown that the number-one fear among Christian parents and Christian leaders is that a secular worldview and sexual immorality will somehow capture the hearts and minds of their kids. We certainly had that fear for our own children. To address that fear, many parents have helped open and develop more Christian schools. They have formed more networks to homeschool their children than ever before. Many have sent their kids off to Christian summer camps. Families have started attending megachurches with top-rated youth programs in unprecedented numbers. The hope of these parents has been to counteract the negative influences of a destructive culture in the lives of their children.

However, these positive steps may have actually caused many parents and educators to drop their guard. It's natural to assume that kids are largely insulated from the influences of a corrupt culture if they live in a Christian home, are involved in a good church, are getting a solid Christian education, and are participating in monitored activities.

Actually, though, our kids are far more exposed to destructive cultural influences today than kids were even ten years ago. The reason for this is because right now we are in the midst of a social-media revolution that is allowing a corrupt and twisted morality to have direct access to our children at much earlier ages than ever before, even in the privacy of our own homes and in their bedrooms. This is the intruder we have been talking about.

The Social-Media Revolution

The culture influenced the previous generation through various media such as radio, TV, videos, magazines, and so on. If a parent monitored what his or her child listened to, watched, and read, there was somewhat of an assurance that a child could be insulated from the negative effects of a destructive culture. However, today's social-media revolution has changed everything. Our culture intrudes upon your children through channels that barely existed a decade ago. For example, compare media growth (based on the general U.S. population) over the last decade.

In 2000	In 2010–2011
2.7 hours per week spent online by the average person	18 hours per week spent online by the average person
100 million daily Google searches	2 billion daily Google searches
12 billion e-mails sent daily	247 billion e-mails sent daily
12,000 active blogs	141 million active blogs
0 iTunes downloads	10 billion iTunes downloads[1]
0 tweets on Twitter	25 billion tweets on Twitter[2]
0 YouTube videos seen daily	4 billion YouTube videos seen daily[3]
0 hours of YouTube videos uploaded every minute	60 hours of YouTube videos uploaded every minute[4]
0 people on Facebook	845 million active users on Facebook[5]
0 articles on Wikipedia	20 million articles on Wikipedia

More than 250 million new people were added to Facebook in 2010, with 30 billion pieces of content shared each month.[6] If Facebook were a country, it would have the world's third-largest population.

Approximately 20 million minors are on Facebook. Of those, 7.5 million are younger than 13 years old, and 5 million are younger than 10 years old.[7] It is estimated that Facebook will soon reach 90 percent of all social-network users and 57.1 percent of all U.S. Internet users. By 2013, 62 percent of Internet users and half of the U.S. population are expected to be on Facebook.[8]

In regard to video content, eMarketer estimates that of the 50 million U.S. children under 12, nearly 12 million—about 25 percent—"were online video viewers in 2011." The estimate skyrockets to 70 percent by 2015.[9] According to Harris Interactive, in 2010, the number of children under 12 years old who spent at least one hour a day online increased from 61 percent to 76 percent.[10]

The Internet has surpassed TV as kids' media of choice.[11] A study by the U.S. Department of Education shows that 27 percent of all four- to six-year-olds are on the Internet.[12] Today kindergarteners are learning on iPads, not chalkboards.

The social-media revolution is connecting us in positive ways never before imagined 10 or 20 years ago. Yet all this ability to connect and have people connect to your children may cause you to feel uncomfortable. And it should. There is an alarming downside to the instant accessibility this culture has to your children.

Intrusive Immorality

As parents and Christian leaders, we want our young people to embrace a biblical sexual morality. We want them to enjoy sex as God designed them to enjoy it within the context of marriage. And just 10 or 15 years ago, we as parents, pastors, or Christian educators had a good measure of control over what type of things our young people saw or heard that shaped their view of sex. We could say, "We don't watch those kinds of TV programs in our home; nor do we read those types of books." There were certain controls we could put in place to insulate our children from damaging influences. When our children wanted to visit neighbors or friends, we tried to limit it to people with our same convictions.

But today we have, by and large, lost control of the controls. That is because a perverted morality is just one click away from our children. With just one keystroke on a smartphone, iPad, or laptop, your child can open up some of the worst pornography and sexually graphic content you can imagine. Just a few decades ago pornographic magazines were sold behind store counters and placed in paper bags. Most adult men didn't even want to be seen carrying such a magazine out of a store. Today pornography is available to anyone, including your kids and teenagers.

Immoral sexual content is reaching many, if not the majority, of our children. According to research from Family Safe Media, the average age of the first Internet exposure to pornography is nine years old.[13] And there are plenty of sites to be exposed to. There are over 5 million pornographic sites available today with over 68 million search requests daily.[14] More than 2.5 billion porn e-mails are circulated every day.[15]

A 2009 survey of 29,000 North American university students confirmed that 51 percent of males and 32 percent of females first viewed pornography before their teenage years.[16] A journal article, "The Nature and Dynamics of Internet Pornography Exposure for Youth," reports that 93 percent of boys and 62 percent of girls are exposed to Internet porn before they are 18 years old. Eighty-three percent of boys and 57 percent of girls have seen group sex. Sixty-nine percent of boys and 55 percent of girls have viewed homosexual or lesbian acts. Thirty-nine percent of boys and 23 percent of girls have been exposed to sexual acts depicting bondage.[17]

According to a study cited in the *Washington Post*, more than 11 million teenagers view Internet porn on a regular basis.[18] A Focus on the Family poll revealed that 47 percent of families said that pornography is a problem in their home.[19] These were largely Christian families responding to the poll.

Who Is Concerned About This?

In contrast to the situation several decades ago, most of our young people see little or no problem with viewing pornography. Overall, studies show that 67 percent of young men and 49 percent of young women 18 to 26 years of age consider viewing pornography as acceptable behavior.[20]

Of course, as a concerned parent, you no doubt warn your children and teens to stay away from "sex sites." As a responsible and proactive parent, you may even install Internet filtering and monitoring software on your computers, as you should.

Yet what happens when your children visit their friends and they turn on their cell phones? Do the parents of your children's friends have sexually explicit material blocked from all their electronic devices? The problem is that sexually oriented and perverted material through cyberspace is everywhere, and it is difficult to avoid, even when you try to block it.

Further, more than 1.5 billion pornographic peer-to-peer downloads occur each month,[21] and most are not detected by "family filters." (*Peer-to-peer* is from one computer directly to another computer.) An entire pornographic video can be downloaded by a child, often without detection by parents.

Because of the massive amount of sexually perverted material available today, the sheer overexposure, no matter how infrequent, tends to desensitize a young person. Rather than gaining an understanding of what sex is really for, why it comes with boundaries, and how it can bring intimacy and joy in a committed marriage relationship, young people tend to think everyone is doing whatever they want sexually without consequences. This is clearly the impression given through cyberspace.

Most young people have been so desensitized to sexually explicit material that they see no problem with joking, posting, or texting about provocative sex. Do you realize that 4 out of 10 teens are posting sexually suggestive messages? And another 39 percent of teen boys and 38 percent of teen girls say they have had sexually suggestive text messages or e-mails—originally meant for someone else—shared with them.[22]

No doubt, it seems to our kids that the entire world around them, including their peers, is into premarital sex. We, of course, know that not everyone is "doing it"; yet our kids' perception becomes their reality. The irony is, many Christian adults tend to think *none* of their kids are involved sexually, while their own kids think *everyone* else is "doing it." These contradictory viewpoints are widespread.

Recently, I (Josh) did a two-hour seminar on "The Bare Facts: The Truth About Sex, Love, and Relationships" at the staff conference of an evangelical organization. At an afternoon session, 1800 people showed up with their kids. In the next three days, ten different staff members told me that one of their children (all under the age of 14) had confessed to them that they were addicted to pornography on the Internet. Each parent expressed amazement and had never suspected a thing.

During a recent pastor's conference I was addressing the same topic, and five pastors approached me after a session with their stories:

- Pastor #1: "I just found out that my two sons (ages 14 and 18) are struggling with pornography on the Internet." Then he confessed that he had been addicted to pornography himself for 11 years.

- Pastor #2: "I learned last week that my 17-year-old son just got his girlfriend pregnant and my 15-year-old daughter is also pregnant. What do I do? I'm going to have two grandchildren soon!" He shared that his son regularly viewed pornography.

- Pastor #3 (a youth pastor): "My 14-year-old daughter has been giving oral sex to the boys at her [Christian] school."

- Pastor #4: "I just found my 8-year-old son watching pornography on my office computer."

- Pastor #5: "My 5-year-old son has been looking at pornography since he was 4 years old." The pastor was crushed.

These five conversations happened in the 20-minute time span it took me to get from the podium to my car.

Before I could get into the car, a desperate teenager gripped my arm and said, "Dr. McDowell, would you please pray for me? I've been struggling with pornography for three years and it is destroying me!"

Several years ago, I was invited to speak on sex and relationships at one of the largest and most prestigious evangelical Christian schools in North America. The administration appreciated that I came to speak on that subject, but they made the following request: "We don't want you to mention anything about oral sex," they said, "because we don't have that problem here. If you mention it, our kids will simply start thinking about it and want to do it."

I thought their request was absurd and naive, but out of respect, I honored it. The moment I finished speaking, dozens of kids crowded around me to ask questions. Nearly every question was about oral sex. "Is it sex?" "Is it wrong?" "Can you get an STD from doing it?" and so on.

I wished the school headmaster had been standing there to hear his students. As I walked outside, three guys and two girls, all sophomores, approached me and asked, "Why didn't you talk about oral sex?"

I avoided telling them that I had been asked not to talk on the subject. Instead, I asked them, "Why? Is oral sex a problem here?" And they said, "No, not really." I replied, "That's good," to which they responded, "No, it's not a problem for kids to do, because everyone is doing it." (This was an exaggeration.)

I asked them to explain. "Well," they stated, "at our school when a guy wants oral sex, he walks up to a girl and says, "Would you like a taco?" That was their code word for oral sex. They went on to explain, "If she agrees, they go into some room right here at school and perform oral sex. But then the boy is obligated after school to take the girl to Taco Bell to buy her a taco."

According to these kids, oral sex was commonplace. According to the school leadership, "We don't have that kind of problem here." The disconnect between what many parents and Christian leaders believe their young people are doing, and what kids are actually doing, is vast. Sure, we don't want to think our sons and daughters are involved in sexual activity of any kind and are being brainwashed with a distorted view of sex. But the truth is, if we are not proactive to counter what our kids are exposed to, chances are they will be captured by a destructive culture.

So What Can You Do?

It seems that it would be ideal if we could reverse the social-media explosion. But we can't, nor should we even try. In fact, in the last 12 months, some estimate more than 200 million people were confronted with the claims of Christ on the Internet. Social media themselves are not the real culprit here. They are simply the vehicle that can bring either positive or destructive influences into the lives of our kids.

Escaping to a remote island where only committed Christians live might seem like a definitive solution. Then we could raise our kids where no secular culture could influence them. But that isn't a realistic alternative any more than reversing the media revolution we are experiencing. So what can we do?

1. We must acknowledge the reality that kids are being negatively influenced with a distorted view of sex by the culture. We can't live in denial of what is really happening. It is like one young mother said, "It feels as if we are trying to raise our kids in the center of Las Vegas." So the first step to a solution is seeing the problem as it truly exists.

2. We need to counter the distorted and perverted views about sex our kids are hearing and seeing with the correct and healthy understanding of sex. Let's say you are among those parents who have one or more children over the age of seven. And let's say you are just now getting around to talking to them about sex. By now your kids have already got their sex education from the outside culture. And in all probability their understanding of sex is distorted and quite different than what you had hoped.

In this case, you will need to *reintroduce* your kids to a whole new concept of what sex is and why God created it. In many respects you will need to deconstruct the distorted concepts of sex they have adopted and represent an understanding based on God's design. If your children are much younger you may still have time to get to them before the culture does. But you must start with them at a very young age.

Teaching kids God's idea of sex means that we as parents and Christian leaders must first clearly understand why he created us as sexual beings in the first place. We must know the real purpose of sex, what sexual purity actually means, why there are boundaries around sex, and how a loving relationship is the cornerstone in teaching God's view of sex. With this type of foundational understanding you will have a biblical context for introducing or reintroducing your children to what sex is all about. This will give you the biblical basis to raise your family to embrace a healthy (godly) perspective of sex. And that is what we will address in part one of this book, "Sex Is God's Design."

3. We must actively guide, lead, and instruct our kids in God's perspective of sex. And to do that we offer you valuable and practical tools in part two, "Tips and Ideas for Your Conversations." These short chapters have insights, examples, answers, and ways to deal with so many issues that you either have encountered or soon will encounter. We will discover together the wonderful opportunities to introduce or reintroduce God's wonderful gift of sex to your kids.

As parents we (Josh and Dottie) didn't do it perfectly. Perfect parents don't exist. But we are grateful for the wonderful opportunity we had to impart to our children God's plan for sex. All four of our kids are married now and have children of their own. And it is thrilling to watch them successfully passing on a biblical view of sex to their own children—our grandchildren. Be encouraged—your biblical values on love and sex can be passed on to the next generation. And we hope the pages that follow will help you in your effort to do just that.

Part One

Sex Is God's Design

Chapter 2

Sex: Created Within the Context of God's Image

This was a day like no other. Everything seemed perfect, as if nothing could ever be better. It was a paradise of grasses and flowers with animals of all kinds living under a canopy of clouds and sky... everything painted a breathtaking canvas of perfection and beauty. But something was still missing in this Garden of Eden. Because Adam, the first human, walked in this paradise without a human companion.

God declared, "It is not good for the man to be alone" (Genesis 2:18). Here in this perfect world, where sin had not yet brought shame or heartache, there was a missing piece. Adam had a great relationship with God. He had the perfect job of attending to a beautiful garden. He had plenty to eat. Yet deep inside Adam was a void, an aching emptiness he couldn't explain—not until God did something extraordinary.

God placed Adam into a deep sleep. And when the man awoke he experienced something beyond his comprehension—he experienced a creature called *woman*.

Imagine how Adam might have gazed through softly waving

palms to see a face so captivating that he thought he'd be content
never to look at anything else again. Imagine how raptly he watched
her glide toward him with elegance and grace. Her softly sculp-
tured shape and form was like nothing he had seen before. Imagine how fast his heart beat—her beauty, her fragrance, her presence
filling his senses until it took his breath away. Why was he so magi-
cally attracted to her? What was this indefinable hunger to know her
more than what he could see with his eyes? For the first time humans
personally experienced this amazing gift from God called sexuality.

The Bible says this newly created man and woman were naked.
They obviously desired each other physically. They naturally enjoyed
one another sexually. And they did all this without guilt or shame
(see Genesis 2:25). But where did this sexually passionate attraction
to one another come from, and for what reason?

Sexuality Came from Somewhere

The sun's rays and the moon's beams were created by God. He
spoke and the vast oceans, expansive lakes, rushing rivers, and cas-
cading waterfalls materialized. The snow-capped mountains, the
lush forests, the flat prairies, and all the animals that inhabit them
were spoken into existence by God. The earth and all the planets of
the universe burst into being from God's great creative voice. But
sex—that was a different type of creation. That one was on a totally
different level. All creation was spoken into existence by God, but
for humans and human sexuality God did something even more
amazing.

The first chapter of the very first book of the Bible makes it clear:
"God created human beings in his own image. In the image of God
he created them; male and female he created them" (Genesis 1:27).
Rather than simply speaking humans into existence, God personally

formed the first human out of physical elements of the earth and then "breathed the breath of life" into him. This means Adam was more than simply an animal spoken into being. He and all his offspring were living souls with human sexuality created in God's image.

Being created in God's image doesn't mean we look like him, because "God is Spirit, so those who worship him must worship in spirit and in truth" (John 4:24). While it is true that he took on human form in the person of Jesus, God doesn't exist as a material or physical being—he is Spirit. Yet God created us physically, emotionally, spiritually and relationally with godlike characteristics, and that includes our sexuality. We were created by God in his own image, and yet we are sexual beings who are sexually attracted to each other. Is this sexual attraction a God thing that is somehow part of his image?

Some have suggested that the natural male-to-female attraction toward one another is rooted in the reality that within the nature of God reside both female and male characteristics. We know he is neither wholly male nor female in a literal sense even though he characterizes himself in masculine terms. Yet in his masterful design he has created two separate kinds of humans—one male and one female. And therefore the magnetic attraction of man to woman and woman to man might originate in the unity and completeness of a God who bears the characteristics of both male and female. God, so to speak, inherently has both the plus and minus characteristics of male and female, and when the two characteristics are placed separately in the two sexes, they naturally attract each other, like the opposing magnetic poles. The Godhead is one—in unity—and he created the two sexes to be in unity. That at least is one theory of why males and females are so attracted to one another. And it does have some merit.

Scripture teaches us that oneness—unity—is a defining char-acteristic of God. It declares "the LORD is one" (Deuteronomy 6:4 NIV). This singularity of God doesn't contradict that God is Trin-ity, because Scripture is also clear that God is Father, Son, and Holy Spirit. However, this oneness of God demonstrates that a perfect relationship of unity exists within the Godhead. The Father has always been in infinite relationship and unity with the Son. The Son has always been in unity with the Father. And the Holy Spirit has always been in infinite harmony with both the Father and the Son. This perfect oneness isn't something God strives for; it is not some-thing he creates. It is something he *is*. "The Father and I are one," Jesus said. "Realize that the Father is in me, and I am in the Father" (John 10:30,38).

The image of God reflects oneness and unity in perfect relation-ship. His togetherness is a relationship so infinitely loving that it produces an intimate oneness, a bonding, a togetherness, and a con-nectedness unparalleled in the universe. God cannot be separated. He cannot be divided. He exists as an eternal intimate relationship. And it is this capacity for loving, intimate relationships that humans have received from God himself.

The Intimacy Factor

"This explains why a man leaves his father and mother and is joined to his wife, and the two are united into one" (Genesis 2:24). Our desire and need for intimacy in relationship is rooted in the image of God as one. Marriage and marital sex between a man and a woman reflects God's nature of oneness and unity. Sexuality is a beautiful gift from God that gives humans the capacity for an inti-mate, loving relationship.

I (Dottie) have had women share with me how they grew up

believing *sex* was a dirty word. Even within marriage some of them feel guilty for engaging in sex with their husbands. It's clear these women have a distorted view. There is no reason to feel dirty or guilty about sexual relations within the context of marriage. God created sex for married couples to enjoy an intimate connection.

This truth has even been confirmed on a biological level. Researchers have discovered a hormone called *oxytocin*, nicknamed the "cuddle hormone." Oxytocin is a chemical your brain releases during sex and the activity leading up to it. When this chemical is released, it prompts feelings of caring, trust, and deep affection. The same chemical is released when a mother breastfeeds her new baby. The purpose is to create a deep human bond or attachment to the other person.

Every time you have sex with another person, your body has a chemical reaction—the release of oxytocin—that tells you to be intimate with that person. That is one of the primary purposes of sex—to lead to an intimate relationship. God is the one who created the means to meet the human desire for intimacy at a biological level. But that's only part of the whole. Relational intimacy isn't fully achieved by simply engaging in a physical sex act. Human sexuality involves every aspect of a person's being—physical, emotional, spiritual, and relational. And sex is meant to connect us on every level.

Over the years we have encountered scores of married couples wanting to know why they have lost the intimacy in their relationship. They have sex physically, but they are missing a deep love that connects them on every level. It's as if they see sex as a physical pleasure separate from their spiritual, emotional, and relational lives. It is something they do rather than being a way of expressing every aspect of their lives with each other. Reality is, a fantastic sex life isn't the cause of a great relationship. Rather, an intimate, close relationship on every level results in a fantastic sex life.

Most of our kids are also confused about what sex is all about. Many think it's there to simply make them feel physically close to their boyfriend or girlfriend. Sure—sex gives you a physical sense of closeness for a brief moment, but as we've been saying, one of its real purposes is to bring every dimension of a couple together spiritually, emotionally, and relationally for a lifetime. That is why Jesus said, "Since they [a married couple] are no longer two but one, let no one split apart what God has joined together" (Matthew 19:6). So until a man or woman is ready to commit to a lifetime of intimacy, they should not be engaging in an act that is designed to achieve that very thing.

As we raise our children one thing we need to make clear to them is that sex—that attraction between the opposite sex—is God's beautiful gift to each of us. It's not something that is dirty even though some people misuse it and distort his purpose for it. Just because a destructive culture distorts a beautiful thing doesn't mean we act as though it's a plague. We must lift up sex and human sexuality to the high level that God designed it. After all, it came from him—we were created sexual beings in his image.

The Pleasure Factor

God created sex and sexual relations as that bonding agent to deeply connect a man and a woman together spiritually, emotionally, relationally, and physically for a lifetime. But he didn't create this "bonding agent" as a one-time event. The "urge to merge" can be felt as frequently and as often as our appetite for food, perhaps even more so for some.

Intimacy is a very important factor of sex, but engaging in marital sex for sheer pleasure is another. Sex should be a blast for a married man and woman who commit to loving one another for life. That doesn't necessarily mean sexual pleasure will last into old age, but it might. There was an 84-year-old professor who taught a course on human sexuality at a university. One of his students asked how long sex could be enjoyed by couples. He stated, "I don't know, but it's until sometime after 84." Pure and simple, sex is designed for pleasure—to playfully enjoy each other within the bonds of marriage as long as your bodies can handle it.

We realize there are those who disagree with the point that sex is also for pleasure. And we as a couple do not judge those who disagree with us. We respect those who believe sex is an obligation and a duty—we just feel it is our duty to explain that they are missing out on all the great pleasure! And if it helps, we can even back up the claim that having sex in marriage for fun is good by providing Scripture verses.

Sometimes people ask me (Josh), "Do you take the Bible literally?" I quickly reply, "When it comes to the wise advice of Solomon I absolutely do!" Read for yourself:

> *Let your wife be a fountain of blessing for you. Rejoice in the wife of your youth. She is a loving deer, a graceful doe. Let her breasts satisfy you always. May you always be captivated by her love (Proverbs 5:18-19).*

> *You are slender like a palm tree, and your breasts are like its clusters of fruit. I said, "I will climb the palm tree and take hold of the fruit." May your breasts be like grape clusters, and the fragrance of your breath like apples. May your kisses be as exciting as the best wine, flowing gently over lips and teeth (Song of Solomon 7:6-9).*

Now that's my kind of Scripture! Don't let anything (a culture or your past distorted teachings) rob you of the joy God wants you to have in your sex life.

One of the things I (Dottie) did as our kids were growing up was to let them know how much Josh and I enjoyed each other. Of course kids don't want to mentally envision their parents' sexual encounters. But I let my kids know that sexual relations were designed to be a beautiful and enjoyable experience when expressed in the context of marriage. And in very subtle ways I let them know Josh and I enjoyed God's gift a great deal. And by the way, if you need more scriptural reinforcements that God wants sex to be enjoyed within the context of marriage, check out more of the Song of Songs (Song of Solomon).

The Procreation Factor

One of the first things God said to the first couple, Adam and Eve, was, "Be fruitful and multiply" (Genesis 1:28). Now that has to be one of the most enjoyable commands ever to fulfill! And without fulfilling this procreation command, the human race would not continue.

At the beginning of the verse in Genesis it says, "Then God blessed them and said, 'Be fruitful and multiply...'" (Genesis 1:28). The result of having children is clearly a blessing. Solomon said, "Grandchildren are the crowning glory of the aged; parents are the pride of their children" (Proverbs 17:6).

Perhaps there is no greater thrill than to realize that your intimate expression of love toward your spouse has created a precious life that will forever be known as your son or daughter. Sure, there are challenges to birthing and raising a child these days. But what an awesome privilege and blessing it is to have a family.

You as a parent, or a Christian leader responsible to help parents and their kids, want your children to navigate through life without hitting the landmines of pornography, premarital sex, or the heart-ache of broken families and relationships. You truly want your kids to be a blessing to you, to God, and to the world around them. That is what we all want. And one of the first steps to accomplish that is in helping our kids understand that sex is from God, that it is good, and that it is designed for not only procreation but also for their rela-tional intimacy and for their enjoyment. And how you share that is the subject of this entire book.

Our children need to understand how God wants sex to bless their lives and relationships. They need to understand its purpose. But they also need to understand if they are to use it right, they must understand "the rules of engagement." Just as with anything that is truly powerful and dynamic, we must understand how it is supposed to be used. And in the next chapter we will examine how sex is to be experienced within the context of boundaries.

Chapter 3

Sex: Lived Within the Context of Boundaries

It was a warm, dark night, and Justin and his girlfriend Maddie wanted to go swimming. Justin knew that the neighbors down the street were away for an extended time, and they had a beautiful in-ground pool in their backyard. So he and Maddie sneaked behind the neighbor's house, scaled the fence surrounding the pool, and set out to enjoy an evening swim.

Justin threw off his shoes, climbed the diving-board ladder, and before Maddie could even get her shoes and socks off, dove in. He heard her scream just before he lost consciousness.

The neighbors had drained most of the water from the pool so there were only a few feet in the deep end. Unable to see this in the darkness, Justin's dive ended with a shallow splash of water and a sickening crunch of bones. His late-night dive paralyzed him from the neck down for the rest of his life.

This couple wanted nothing more than to enjoy the pleasure of a twosome swim party. The fence marked a boundary—a boundary that implicitly said, "Do Not Enter," "No Trespassing," and "Keep Out." But Justin saw the fence as a killjoy, meant to keep him and his girlfriend from having the fun they wanted. In reality, the fence was meant for his protection.

There Is Pleasure in Sex

In raising your children you have no doubt at some point warned them, "Don't touch the stove" or "Look both ways before you cross the street." You've given them mundane instructions like "Don't forget to brush your teeth." You weren't being a "killjoy"—your directives were meant for your child's benefit. You naturally didn't want them to get burned, be hit by a car, or get even one cavity in a tooth. The negative commands are human-made boundaries— like a fence designed to protect your child from harm.

You have probably been successful in teaching your child certain basics. They have probably learned that touching a hot stove will burn, that stepping in front of a speeding car will do damage, and that cavities will rot away teeth when they aren't brushed consistently. But it is a greater challenge for young people, even adults of any age, to learn that violating God's commands about sexual behavior causes suffering and heartache. And there is a good reason why that is such a challenge.

Touching a hot stove brings instant pain. Getting hit by a speeding car results in immediate damage. But engaging in sex is generally pleasurable whether it's within the boundaries of marriage or not. The physical pleasure of sex can be gratifying regardless of whether it is morally permissible or not. A young person's body doesn't know whether it is married or not.

Reality is, in the heat of the moment sex feels good no matter if it is morally right or wrong. So we are not going to be very successful in teaching our kids that sex before marriage isn't right because it doesn't feel good. They have already been told by numerous outside sources that sex is great almost anytime. And it is generally portrayed in the media as instant pleasure with no long-term negative consequences. So how do we counter that?

Explain How to Maximize Sex

Now, as parents or Christian leaders, what do we say to kids to keep them from doing something? We generally tell them how bad it is and all the negative consequences they'll experience if they do X, Y, or Z. It would seem the last thing we want to say to a young person is how to get the most out of the thing we want them to avoid. Right?

Well, when it comes to sex, our kids need to understand how fantastic and great it is *when it is experienced with the right person at the right time.* In other words, when a person engages in sex within the context God designed, then he or she can enjoy it to the max! When we follow the instructions about how something is designed and the way it is made to work—it works. We simply maximize the benefits of things by using them the way they were designed to be used.

Have you ever tried to take a pet fish on a walk, or grow a palm tree at the North Pole, or simply screw a Phillips screw in with a conventional screwdriver? You will have problems all the way around. Why? Because fish were not created to take walks. They were designed to live in water, not on land. And if a fish is going to enjoy its life as it was meant to be enjoyed, then it has to live where it was created and meant to live—in water.

Palm trees were meant to flourish in perpetually warm weather. They are tropical trees. If they are to live as they were meant to live, they have to stay away from cold climates like the North Pole. Even a simple task like screwing a Phillips screw into a wall becomes hard when you use the wrong screwdriver. If machines, plants, and animals are going to experience maximum function they have to exist according to their design. It's just that simple.

Our kids need to understand that sex is from God for a designed purpose. Sex is a fantastic gift to increasingly deepen a married couple's love life, to bring joy and physical pleasure into their relationship, and to create a loving family of one or more children. If you respect and honor sex for how it was meant to be used then—wow, sex is one of the best things God created.

Let your kids know there is a clear way to enjoy the wonderful gift of sex. It's not something dirty or wrong. It is a beautiful way to bond when one critical guideline is adopted—follow the instructions of how it was designed to be used! Make concerted efforts to let your kids know there is a specific design and a set of instructions that God gave us on how to maximize their sex lives.

"No" Is the *Positive* Answer

Did you ever notice whenever God tells us "no" in his Word he does so out of two loving motivations? He always wants to provide for us and to protect us. Moses acknowledged God's loving motivation when he challenged the nation of Israel:

> *Now, Israel, what does the* LORD *your God require from you, but to fear the* LORD *your God, to walk in all his ways and love him, and to serve the* LORD *your God with all your heart and with all your soul, and to keep the* LORD's *commandments and His statutes w*hich I am commanding you today for your good? (Deuteronomy 10:12-13* NASB*).*

The reason God says no—"don't do this" or "don't do that"— is for our good. The reason he establishes boundaries and puts up the "Keep Out" sign is to provide for us and protect us. Check out Psalm 145. It describes God as a gracious provider and protector. And when it comes to the matter of sex, God also wants to be our provider and protector. But to experience this we must honor the boundaries and prohibition signs for sexual behavior. In other words, we must avoid sexual immorality.

In biblical terms, sexual immorality is all sex that occurs outside of a marriage between one man and one woman (extramarital and premarital sex). Scripture states:

- "You must abstain from...sexual immorality" (Acts 15:29).

- "Run from sexual sin!" (1 Corinthians 6:18).

- "We must not engage in sexual immorality" (1 Corinthians 10:8).

- "Among you there must not be even a hint of sexual immorality...because these are improper for God's holy people" (Ephesians 5:3 NIV).
- "God's will is for you to be holy, so stay away from all sexual sin" (1 Thessalonians 4:3).

Respecting the boundaries of sexual morality and the "Stop" signs for extramarital and premarital sex does bring protection and provision. Here are just a few.

Protection from	Provision for
guilt	spiritual rewards
unplanned pregnancy	optimum atmosphere for child-raising
sexually transmitted diseases	peace of mind
sexual insecurity	trust
emotional distress	true intimacy

Experiencing those benefits definitely maximizes a person's sex life in marriage. For example, as a young couple going together we (Josh and Dottie) made a decision early on to wait until the loving commitment of marriage before expressing ourselves sexually. That commitment meant we would remain sexually faithful to one another after marriage. And we have. Because we both were obedient to God's commands regarding sex, we have been protected from feelings of guilt and have enjoyed an uninterrupted relationship with God.

We never had to go through the heartache of a pregnancy before marriage. Consequently, we did not experience the heart-wrenching ordeal of planning an adoption or struggling with getting married before we were ready because of pregnancy.

We have been protected from the fear that any sexually transmitted disease might come into our marriage bed.

We have been protected from the sexual insecurity that can occur from being compared to past sexual lovers one's spouse may have had. And consequently, we have experienced the provision of trust in our relationship.

We have been protected from the emotional distress that premarital sex can bring and the feelings of betrayal that an extramarital affair can cause. As a result we have enjoyed relational intimacy together unobstructed by breaches of trust or ghosts from the past.

Sex as God designed it was meant to be lived within the context of healthy boundaries—prohibitions before marriage and fidelity after marriage. Following God's design then allows a couple to experience the beauty of sex as it was meant to be experienced. But it is vitally important that our kids understand what these boundaries are and be able to identify them by name. Because these boundaries and limits are what makes the "no" such a positive answer. They are the very reason sex is maximized when we live within them.

Identifying the Boundaries for Sexual Behavior

We've already said that God's boundaries are there to protect us and provide for us. And there are at least three sexual boundaries described in Scripture. Figuratively speaking, these three depict one pathway with two guiding guardrails. And when we walk that path, not straying off to the right or left, we maximize sex as God intended.

The Boundary of Purity

The Bible says, "Marriage should be honored by all, and the marriage bed kept pure" (Hebrews 13:4 NIV). "God's will is for you to be holy, so stay away from sexual sin. Then each of you will control his own body and live in holiness and honor—not in lustful passion... God has called us to live holy lives, not impure lives" (1 Thessalonians 4:3-5,7).

Purity is God's boundary that provides for a maximum sex life and protects us from the negative consequences of sexual immorality. But what does it mean to be pure?

Have you ever had a candy bar that identified itself on the wrapper as "pure milk chocolate"? What about a jar of honey? Some labels read "Pure honey—no artificial sweeteners." Purity of chocolate or honey means there is no foreign substance to contaminate it or to keep it from being what authentic chocolate or honey is supposed to taste like.

To be pure sexually is to "live according to God's original design," without allowing anything to come in to ruin his authentic, perfect plan for sex. You see, sex was designed to be expressed between one husband and one wife. To have more than one sexual partner would be to bring a foreign substance into the relationship, and it would cease to be pure. If you were to drop a dirty pebble into a glass of pure water, it would become adulterated—or impure. A glass of water without any impurities in it is an unadulterated glass of water. God wants our sex lives to be unadulterated.

God's design is that sex be experienced within an unbroken circle, a pure union between two virgins entering into an exclusive relationship. That pure union can be broken even *before* marriage, if one or both of the partners has not kept the marriage bed pure by waiting to have sex until it can be done in the purity of a husband-wife relationship.

And where did this sexual purity come from? From the very image of God himself. God says, "Be holy, for I am holy" (1 Peter 1:16 NASB). "Everyone who has this hope [of glory] in him purifies himself, just as he [God] is pure" (1 John 3:3 NIV). God by nature is holy and pure. "There is no evil in him" (Psalm 92:15). And when we reflect the image of God by remaining sexually pure before marriage and after marriage, we enjoy the protection and provision of sex and experience it as it was meant to be experienced.

The Boundary of Faithfulness

The seventh commandment is "You must not commit adultery" (Exodus 20:13). Jesus made the point that once a man and woman are united as one in marriage they are not to commit adultery but remain faithful to one another. Jesus said, "Let no one split apart what God has joined together" (Mark 10:9). God told Israel, "I hate divorce!…so guard your heart; do not be unfaithful to your wife" (Malachi 2:16).

What couples do at their wedding is commit to be faithful to one another…"to have and to hold, from this day forward, for better, for worse, for richer, for poorer, in sickness and in health, to love and to cherish till death do us part. And hereto I pledge you my faithfulness." Perhaps nothing is more rewarding than to sense someone loves you more than any other and will devote themselves to you for life. *Faithfulness is God's boundary* that provides for a maximum sex life and protects us from the negative consequences of sexual immorality.

My husband (Josh) has traveled away from home for most of our married life. He has had more than one opportunity to be unfaithful to me. But in over 40 years of marriage he has demonstrated a loyalty, a faithfulness, a devoted commitment to only one love and sex relationship in his life. And that is with me. That means the world to me. It deepens my own sense of worth, gives me security, and tells me I am loved. Of all the more than 3 billion women on this planet I am the one-and-only to my lover, Josh. That kind of love is something to cherish.

We were created by God with the desire and longing to be that "one and only" to someone else. It came directly from the very nature of God himself. "Understand…that the LORD your God is indeed God," Moses told the Israelites. "He is the faithful God who keeps his covenant for a thousand generations" (Deuteronomy 7:9). A faithful love commitment is yet another protection and provision boundary for our sex lives.

The Pathway of Love

Sex is to be lived within the boundaries of purity on one side and faithfulness on the other. What that does is provide the solid path for a married couple's sexual relationship. And that pathway is love.

Most kids growing up in a Christian home have a moral standard. If you have a teenager he or she probably believes that kids having sex with anyone, anytime is definitely wrong. And, of course, you should be proud he or she holds that view. But there's a catch.

Most kids from good churches and Christian families feel that it is somehow different if two people are in a committed relationship where "true love" is involved. Then engaging in sex before marriage seems justified because "love makes it right."

I (Josh) shock many parents and church leaders when I say that I agree, in a way, with today's young people—I believe that true love *does* make it right. Now, before you e-mail me a complaint, hear me out. True love *is* the biblical standard for sex. The problem is, most youth are working from a counterfeit standard of love—one that says love permits sex without the boundaries of purity and fidelity.

What we need to understand is *God's definition of love.* In 1 Corinthians, the apostle Paul gives a good description of what love does and does not do:

> *Love is patient and kind. Love is not jealous or boastful or proud or rude. It does not demand its own way. It is not irritable, and it keeps no record of being wronged. It does not rejoice about injustice but rejoices whenever the truth wins out (1 Corinthians 13:4-6).*

But that really doesn't define what love is.

Paul wrote that "love does no wrong to others" (Romans 13:10). Instead, we are to treat all people as we would like to be treated. Remember the Golden Rule? "Do to others," Jesus commanded, "whatever you would like them to do to you" (Matthew 7:12). Paul put it this way: "Each of you should look not only to your own interests, but also to the interests of others" (Philippians 2:4 NIV). Now we begin to see that real love isn't self-seeking.

Now check out how Scripture commands a husband to love his wife.

> *Husbands ought to love their wives as they love their own bodies. For a man who loves his wife actually shows love for*

himself. No one hates his own body but feeds and cares for it, just as Christ cares for the church (Ephesians 5:28-29).

What kind of love is that? A love that feeds, nourishes, and provides for the other and also cares for, cherishes, and protects him or her.

With these verses and others as a guide, we can then define true love like this:

Love is making the security, happiness, and welfare of another person as important as your own.

When a person loves another person like that, he or she will allow the boundaries of purity and faithfulness to guide their sex life, because that provides for their happiness and protects them from harm. Love—true love—will wait until marriage to engage in sex and remain pure and faithful within marriage. So in that respect, true love does make it right.

And where does this love originate? From God, "for God is love" (1 John 4:8). God's definition of love is the kind of love that protects the loved one from harm and provides for his or her good. His love is giving and trusting, secure and safe, loyal and forever. And because its priority is to protect and provide for the loved one, his kind of love will not do things that are harmful to the security, happiness, and welfare of another person.

Isn't that the path you want your kids to walk down? Isn't the commitment to purity and fidelity the boundaries you want your young people to embrace? It isn't necessarily easy to instill these truths in our kids with a culture around them that says otherwise. But we are here to say it is possible. You don't have to sit your kids down and try to teach them these truths in classroom fashion. In fact, that can be rather counterproductive. But there is a way to instill God's plan for sex within your kids. There is an approach that will promote a positive response from them. And many parents and Christian leaders simply overlook it. That is the subject of the next chapter.

Chapter 4

Sex: Taught Within the Context of Relationships

He rushed up to me and squeezed my arm. I turned. He spoke without introducing himself. "Josh, what do I do about my family?"

I had just finished speaking to over 600 pastors in the Philippines about "How to Be a Hero to Your Kids." This particular pastor explained to me that his three children—17, 13, and 10 years of age—were considered to be "the worst kids in the church."

"I've done everything I know to do," he said. "I have preached God's Word to them constantly. I've made them memorize Scripture. They know what is expected of them, but they are rebelling. What do I do?"

There was a sense of desperation in this father's voice. He was trying in every way to get his kids to live within the boundaries of God's instructions. He wanted them to experience the protection and provision of obedience. We all want the same for our kids too.

I touched him on his shoulder and looked directly into his eyes.

"Brother, my advice to you is to forget the rules."

"What?" he responded in disbelief. "That's what's wrong—they're not obeying any rules. They don't even think they need to!"

"I know what you're saying," I told him, "but I repeat, lay off emphasizing the rules."

On the surface that doesn't seem like good advice, does it? We all know that rules are important because they provide the boundaries or guidelines for our actions. But that is only the tip of the iceberg, so to speak. We need to understand what brings about real change in our kids' behavior. Because that is what we want in the first place—to guide our kids to make right choices, and when they don't we want to lead them back on the right path. But how do we do that? Dottie and I have found the charts on the following pages and their explanations key in helping us guide our own kids to make right moral choices.

We know that each of our actions and all of our behavior is fostered by something. That something is our values. Moral choices are actually dictated by the values we hold. But what forms our values? Our values are formed out of our beliefs. Each of us comes to believe certain things are true or not true about the world around us. Those beliefs form our values and our values drive our behavior (see diagram).

What we believe can also be referred to as our *worldview*. What is a worldview? Simply stated, it's how we view our world. A worldview is what we assume to be true about the basic makeup of our world. It is the lens through which we see the world. It's like our mental map of reality. So why, for example, do 67 percent of young men and 49 percent of young women consider viewing pornography as acceptable behavior?[1] Their values tell them it's okay because their worldview (their beliefs) has adopted pornography as an acceptable expression of sexuality. Certain beliefs have molded their values, and their values drive their actions.

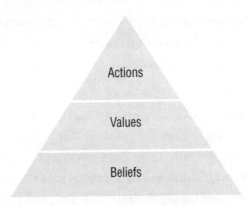

So if our pastor friend from the Philippines simply addresses the action or behavior of his three children, just how far will he get? Oh, he might alter certain behavior with rules or restrictions for a time. But lasting change has to begin on a much deeper level. Many parents, as we stated earlier, homeschool their children or send them to Christian schools, youth group, or Christian summer camp in hopes of changing or molding their behavior. Their hope is that their kids will be taught the right things so they will believe God's truth about love and sex and what is right and wrong. Then perhaps they will make right moral choices. That all may be fine and good—but we are here to say, if teaching your kids to believe the truth is all that you do, it won't be good enough.

The Missing Foundation

Not long ago, I (Josh) was speaking at a large church in the Midwest. The church had just completed a building project and moved into their large, new facility. As I approached the entrance, I noticed a huge banner hanging across the building. It read, "We preach the truth—and the truth only!"

Now of course we are to teach our kids God's truth—that's how they adopt correct beliefs and form a biblical worldview. But I've heard enough similar statements to be suspicious when people talk about the "truth only." So my first thought on seeing the banner was, *If that sign means what I suspect it means, this church is doomed to failure.*

A lot of parents are caught in this same trap. They think they have gone deep enough if they can get their kids to believe God's truth, because then they will hold the right values and do the right things. But this approach is doomed to failure because it is missing the key ingredient that makes God's truth come alive and transform a person's life. And that key is *relationship!*

King David said, "Declare me innocent, O LORD, for I have acted with integrity...I have lived according to your truth" (Psalm 26:1,3). When we only quote verse 1 and the latter part of verse 3, as we have done here, we overlook the very context that truth is to live within. You see, God's truth is always given to us from a loving God who has our best interest at heart. Let's read the whole of verse 3.

For I am always aware of your unfailing love and I have lived according to your truth (Psalm 26:3).

David was constantly aware of the unfailing love of God and the relational connection to him. He saw God's truth within the context of a loving Father who cared about his child. He would later pray, "Teach me your ways, O LORD, that I may live according to your truth," acknowledging that "your love for me is very great" (Psalm 86:11,13). David saw a direct relationship between knowing and loving God and then living in a way to please his loving Father. He had discovered that his right living was empowered by God's unfailing love toward him. The apostle John discovered that power as well when he said, "We love, because He first loved us" (1 John 4:19 NASB).

It's true, as we have stated before, that beliefs shape our values and values drive our actions. Yet the reality is that we all interpret what we believe about God, ourselves, and all of life through our relationship experiences. King David had it right—correct actions come out of embracing God's truth (beliefs and values), and it is all powered by the unfailing love of God (relationship).

All that your young people have learned—everything they know, even *how* they learned it—has come out of a relationship with someone or something. We don't often think of it that way, but much of what each of us is today is a direct result of who we are related to and how. And it is out of these relationships that we establish our beliefs—our worldview. Loving relationships are the fertile ground in which your young people's beliefs grow that shape their values that drive their actions (see diagram).

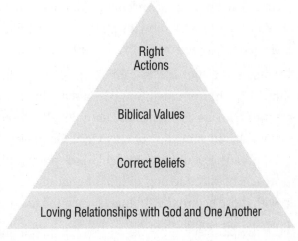

Right
Actions

Biblical Values

Correct Beliefs

Loving Relationships with God and One Another

Why are relationships so important to developing right beliefs, values, and actions? Because we were created that way. The relational

God of the universe planted deep within each of us an identifying marker or distinguishing characteristic of his own likeness—and that was the capacity for loving relationships. We know that from Scripture (Genesis 1:26-27). And recently medical science has confirmed that truth in the development of the structure of the brain.

A number of years ago Dartmouth Medical School commissioned a scientific study of young people. The project, which was called "Hardwired to Connect," analyzed the results of more than 260 studies of youth. The report stated that 100 percent of all the studies they analyzed showed that from the moment a baby is born his or her brain is physically, biologically, and chemically hardwired to connect with others in relationships.[2] This is why highly respected Dr. Allan Schore of the UCLA School of Medicine said, "We are born to form attachments. Our brains are physically wired to develop in tandem with another through emotional communication before words are spoken."[3] That shouldn't surprise us, since we were created in the image of a relational God. Yet far too often we convey rules and truth apart from loving relationships. We, like our two pastor friends, "preach the truth and the truth only."

In Ephesians, the apostle Paul said to "speak the truth in love" (Ephesians 4:15). The truth was always designed to be taught within the context of a loving relationship. Paul said, "We loved you so much that we shared with you not only God's Good News but our own lives, too" (1 Thessalonians 2:8). Paul wasn't promoting a "truth only" approach; he was teaching within the context of a living relationship with those he loved. And that is when the truth took root and people's actions changed.

In fact, without healthy relationships, all attempts to instill beliefs, values, and right actions will be ineffective because they are detached from the necessary elements of personal love and care. It is his personal love and care that God uses to help a person make right moral choices. That is why truth without relationships most often leads to rejection, and discipline or rules without relationships often lead to anger and resentment. But when you place truth within the context of loving relationships, you almost always get a positive response. Why was King David living according to God's truth? Because he was constantly aware of his heavenly Father's "unfailing love"—truth within the context of loving relationships.

Seeing Is Believing

Teaching our kids the truth, what is right and what is wrong about sex, within the context of relationships is vital. Our young people will most likely need to correct their actions—avoid pornography, resist sexual pressure, live within the boundaries of purity and faithfulness, and express love as God defines it. And they will be much more receptive to those instructions—and in fact they will be empowered to live accordingly—as they sense your unfailing love. But they need more than to feel your love; they need to see it lived out before them.

The apostle John said, "Let's not merely say that we love each other; let us show the truth by our actions" (1 John 3:18). For our kids to embrace our beliefs, adopt our values, and make right moral choices, they need to also see truth modeled in our own lives.

When we (Josh and Dottie) saw unhealthy attitudes or wrong actions in our children we of course corrected them. But we learned that our efforts really weren't effective unless our kids could answer yes to three very important questions. Their answers told us whether we were being the right kind of model or not. So when I (Josh) saw something that Kelly did wrong that definitely needed to be addressed, I would ask these questions:

1. "Kelly, do you know that I love you?"

2. "Do you know that I love your mother?"

3. "When you get married, do you want in marriage and love and sex and family life what I have with your mom and you kids?"

If she would answer yes to each of those questions I knew I was in a great position to guide her. I could say, "Kelly, what you are doing can rob you in the future of the kind of things you see me enjoying in my own marriage." Because my daughter was seeing a model of relationships she could believe in, she was far more receptive to my instructions. If our kids don't see it, it will be hard for them to believe it.

The apostle Paul said, "Pattern your lives after mine, and learn from those who follow our example" (Philippians 3:17). The word *example* in the Greek is *tupos,* which means a pattern or model to be replicated or reproduced. Paul was saying that his life was a model to be followed. Your life and ours are also to be a model for our kids to follow. No, we aren't perfect. In fact, there is no such thing as perfect parents. But even in our imperfections we can model humility and be people who seek forgiveness when we're wrong.

I (Dottie) remember a time when Josh and I were in a heated discussion in earshot of the kids. At one point in the argument Josh got quite animated. He threw a folder down on the table and said, "I'm out of here." He then stormed out the door and drove off. None of this went unnoticed by the rest of the family.

But it wasn't long before he was back. He called everyone in for a meeting. In front of all the kids he told me how wrong he had been. He said he was sorry that he'd hurt me emotionally and sought my forgiveness. He then turned to the kids and told them how disrespectful he had been to their mother and sought their forgiveness.

Now, Josh's earlier actions were far from a perfect model, but he was, nonetheless a great model of what you do when you blow it.

Believe it or not, your young people need to see you fail and humbly seek forgiveness as well as see you as a model of right living. Paul explained how he had brought people to God "by my message and by the way I lived before them" (Romans 15:18 NLT). It takes both our words of truth within the context of relationships and our lives as a model. We "show the truth by our actions" (1 John 3:18).

The Father Connection...or Lack Thereof

Johns Hopkins Medical School commissioned a study of 1337 medical doctors who had graduated from their institution. They were interested in childhood family relationships as a factor for certain conditions and diseases. It turned out that mental illness and major cancers were clearly related to lack of closeness to one's parents, especially the father.[4]

When I read that study I was shocked. I called Johns Hopkins Medical School and got in touch with the researchers of the study. I wanted to find out why the lack of closeness to one's father was such a key factor. It took the researchers only about three minutes to convince me why that was the case. They said anyone with a disconnected relationship with their father is more likely to have increased stress in life, and stress is the primary contributing factor in the conditions mentioned.

These and other studies were landmark findings back in the early and mid-1980s. Many studies followed that closely tracked previous studies' indications that relationships and our physical health are interrelated. As recently as February 2012 *Time* magazine reported,

Studies have shown that people with close social networks have lower blood pressure, lower levels of stress hormones

*and more robust immune systems than those without. In
2010, scientists at Brigham Young University analyzed data
gathered from more than 300,000 people. They found that
having poor social connections can raise the risk of premature death as high as that from a smoking habit and even
higher than that from obesity.*[5]

Kids need the loving relationships of their mom and dad to
grow up healthy physically, spiritually, emotionally, and relationally,
which will lead to right choices. And the father connection is vital.

Maria Kefalas, a sociologist who studies marriage and family
issues, coauthored a seminal book on low-income mothers called
*Promises I Can Keep: Why Poor Women Put Motherhood Before Mar-
riage*. She says, "Women always tell me, 'I can be a mother and a
father to a child,' but it's not true. Growing up without a father has
a deep psychological effect on a child. The mom may not need that
man, but her children still do."[6]

Columbia University did an extensive study on how a two-parent
biological family and a single-parent family headed by a mother
affect a teen's involvement in drugs, alcohol, and violence. They
reported that a child raised by a single-parent mother is 30 percent
more likely to get involved in drugs, alcohol, and violence than a
child in a supportive two-parent home.[7] Relationships within the
family with the mom and especially the dad make all the difference
in the world to how a child acts out.

God designed us as relational beings. We all need the unfailing
love of a mother and a father and the abiding friendships of others.
And if we don't get those relational connections we suffer the consequences, especially when we lack a father connection.

We are making a special point about the need for fathers to make a
deep relational connection with their kids. It's not that men have less of

a desire to connect with their children than moms—it's just that most men don't intuitively know how. That is why we devoted an entire book to the subject, entitled *The Father Connection*. We wanted to help dads know how to better connect on a deep level with their sons and daughters.* But the fact that kids are crying out for their fathers should not be seen as a negative reflection on you mothers.

For the most part, studies and our own observations show that you moms are doing it right. Most kids in many respects take their mothers for granted. They sense mom is going to be there for them, to listen to them, to hurt with them, to sympathize with them. But with dad it's another matter. Kids generally don't feel that same relational security with their father. And it negatively impacts them. Most fathers could learn so much from their wives if they would just listen.

And if you are a single mom, let us say this to you: You are doing a far better job with your kids than you think. No, you can't model before your kids a woman's love for a man or a man's love for a woman. But you can be there for your children with all the God-given nurturing and love and support that he gives you. Your kids know you have it rough and somehow know you are going the extra mile every single day.

Also consider this: If your children's father is no longer around or is not a suitable dad, look for mature, godly men in your church who can provide a positive role model of Christian manhood for your kids. Perhaps another dad would be willing to include your kids in family outings or make special efforts to befriend and talk with them. A father figure has a tremendous influence in a child's life. And in families where the father is absent, it's wise to try filling this void with a friend who can serve as a positive role model to your kids.

---

* We encourage you to obtain *The Father Connection*. There is more information about it in the back of this book.

And for all moms: You, more than anyone else, will determine how your children see their father. You have enormous power either to support Dad in his love toward his children or to undermine him and make him look incompetent in their eyes. Encourage your husband in his attempts at fathering. He needs it. Be supportive in your words to him and to your children. He needs you more than he probably realizes. So be patient, be wise, and continue to encourage him to be there for the kids.

Have You Hugged Your Kid Lately?

When your child reaches the teenage years it may seem he or she doesn't want the physical and emotional affection of Mom or Dad. But perhaps more than any time in their life a teenager needs to experience the "unfailing love" of his or her parents.

A young girl wrote a song about her absentee dad, talking about wearing his old clothes. She dreamed of another dad, one who would never abandon her, one who would hold her.

That young girl grew up to record that song under the title "Confessions of a Broken Heart." She would perform in movies, be in and out of jail, go to rehab, and struggle "getting her act together." And so when you look beyond the erratic behavior of actor, songwriter, and musical artist Lindsay Lohan, you see a girl in search of her father's love.

An extraordinarily talented five-year-old boy was rehearsing with his four brothers. The singing brothers were practicing for an upcoming TV special. Their father was guiding them through a number, and they weren't getting their parts just right. The little five-year-old wanted a clarification so he started to ask a question. "Daddy," he began. But instantly his father interrupted him and sternly stated, "I'm not your father now—I'm your manager, and don't you ever forget it." And little Michael Jackson never did.

A few years before his death Michael was speaking to some 800 students at Oxford University, promoting his newly formed foundation Help the Children. About 15 minutes into his presentation he began to weep almost uncontrollably. After a few minutes he regained his composure and seemingly out of nowhere said, "I just wanted a dad. I wanted a father to show me love. But I never once heard my father say, 'Michael, I love you.'"[8]

More than fortune or fame, more than peer acceptance or anything else your kids could dream of, they want to know you are there for them with "unfailing love." No, you don't toss out the rules or lower the boundaries of protection and provision. They need the boundaries to feel secure. But they need those rules and boundaries within the context of your loving relationship. The power of your love toward them will be the motivating factor to make right moral choices.

When you finish reading these words, go to your child or teenager and surprise them with a hug. As you wrap your arms around them let them hear your words, "I love you." And then commit to letting them see your love modeled before them every day. As you do, you will be convincing their emotions that you are there for them with an "unfailing love." Your loving relationship can empower them to believe right, embrace the right values, and live right.

Obviously this is easier said than done. We as parents and Christian leaders may know it is vitally important to build a rich relationship with each of our kids. Yet knowing *how* to do that is another story and many more books. But rather than just stating the need for it we would like to provide at least the basics for relationship building. Much of what we share in the next chapter is drawn from our book *How to Be a Hero to Your Kids*. Since we wrote that book our kids have grown up and started families of their own. So we asked them to share how some of the relational building blocks we attempted to implement affected them. Read on.

Chapter 5

The 7 A's: The Building Blocks
of Relationships

"All right—guarantee me that if I build the right kind of relationship with my kids they will do the right things, make the right choices, and live a life I'll be proud of."

We wish we could. We wish we could say that following the best advice on how to connect relationally with your kids will forever protect them from the heartache of wrong choices and provide them with true happiness. But we can't.

After all your best efforts, your kids may still reject you and your values. But we can say this: By making every effort to build a healthy relationship with your kids and by providing wise information about sex, your chances are much higher. By taking the right steps you are giving your kids a fighting chance of making it successfully through the sexual land mines the enemy has laid before them.

Following is a brief summary of what we call the "7 A's: The Building Blocks of Relationships." Apply these and your kids will be more receptive to what you have to say because they will know and feel that you truly care.*

---

* For a complete treatment of each "A," see the book *How to Be a Hero to Your Kids*, which is described in the back of this book.

1. Approach Your Child's World

"It didn't work, Josh," a father lamented to me. "I took time to be with my son and it was a total failure."

"What did you do together?" I asked.

"Well, I love to golf," he said, "so I took him golfing with me and it was a disaster."

"Does your son like to golf?" I inquired.

"No, but I do," he responded.

This father brought his son into his own world of golf—a world his son didn't like—with a disastrous result. Why? Because the son knew all his father cared about is what "Dad wanted to do." On the other hand, *when we approach our young people's world, we say to them, "I care about you and what you are interested in."*

> *I'm Kelly, the oldest of the McDowell children. Now married with a career of my own I look back on how my parents entered my world. I remember at one point three of us children were playing soccer, all on different teams. There were often six games a week. Yet my mom drove us to every game. I just can't imagine how that could be fun as a mother. Yet every time we left for a game or practice, Mom would always say, "Yeah! We have soccer today. It's going to be so fun to cheer for you." That sure told us she cared about us and our interests.*
>
> *I also remember when I was into snowboarding. My dad took me and my sister to a ski resort to try out our new snowboards. We figured Dad was just going to watch since he didn't ski. But during one of our runs riding up the ski lift I saw Dad on the towrope! My jaw dropped. Dad had never skied in his life, but he wanted to surprise us at the top by*

skiing down with us. That has always stuck with me. Fortunately he didn't break any legs, but it sure spoke volumes to my sister and me. Dad approached our world and that really told us he cared.

The National Campaign to Prevent Teen Unplanned Pregnancy made this appeal to parents: "Be supportive and be interested in what interests them. Attend their sports events; learn about his hobbies; be enthusiastic about her achievements, even the little ones; ask them questions that show you care and want to know what is going on in their lives."[1] And when you do, it opens them up to hear from you, learn from you, and follow your example.

2. Accept Your Child

It was like it was all a dream. I (Dottie) sat there in silence, steam rising from the hood, crushed metal all around me. Was I hurt? Was anyone else hurt? I was just 16 and I had totaled my dad's car.

Naturally I wasn't looking forward to telling my dad what I had just done to his car. What would he say? "Dorothy, what in the world have you done?" or "Weren't you watching the road?" or "How fast were you going anyway?" or "Young lady, do you know how much this is going to cost me?" But Dad said nothing like that. The first words out of his mouth were: "Oh, Dorothy, I'm so glad you weren't hurt!" Over and over Dad just told me how glad he was I was safe. He never once scolded me or lamented the loss of the car. I never forgot it—my dad accepted me even as an immature 16-year-old driver.

When we accept our young people for who they are, we give them a sense of security. Acceptance deals with embracing people for who they are, rather than what they do. When your kids feel accepted without condition, they are more likely to be vulnerable and transparent, opening up greater trust between you. Growing up I felt accepted for just being me. And it created a secure feeling in me that no matter what happened, I'd be loved.

The apostle Paul tells us to "accept each other just as Christ has accepted you" (Romans 15:7). And how does Christ accept you? Unconditionally, right where you are, warts and all. Sure, God wants you to turn away from wrong and make the right choices. But your failures don't affect his love and acceptance of you, because you are his son or daughter. Doesn't that give you a phenomenal sense of security? And doesn't knowing your heavenly Father is not judgmental make it easier to talk to him? Your kids will feel the same way toward you as you increasingly demonstrate you accept them for who they are without condition.

3. Be Available to Your Child

Are you busy? Do you at times feel rushed? Are there not enough hours in a day to do what needs to get done? We all seem to live a fast-paced life these days.

I (Josh) cannot tell you how many times I have allowed my hectic schedule to delay my time with my children. "Not now, Sean, I have a talk to prepare. We'll talk later." "Katie, I have an appointment downtown...we'll need to talk after I'm done." "Heather, maybe later, I need to pack for the airport." "Kelly, I'm pretty exhausted right now, how about after dinner?" Every time I said things like that, I was communicating to my kids that they were not as important as whatever was on my agenda. It breaks my heart when I think about it now.

The way our kids spell love is "T-I-M-E." And *when we make ourselves available to our children we give them a sense of importance.* When we put them off we are in essence saying, "I love you, but other things still come ahead of you."

Life with all its demands doesn't allow us to drop everything every time and give our kids the attention they want. But we need to let them know they are extremely important to us, and giving them our time is one of the best ways to do that.

> *I'm Katie, the third in line of the McDowell children. My dad traveled a lot and wasn't always available in person. But I remember so many phone calls with him. I remember going on the road with him during school breaks and in the summer. And when he was home it seemed like he always picked me up from school. Once, he picked me up in a horse-drawn carriage and took me out for a banana split. Even when a parent's schedule is hectic and full there are ways to make our kids feel they are important. I am sure motivated to make time for my own family.*

4. Affirm Your Child

> *I'm Heather, the youngest of the McDowell children. During high school, I tended to be on the emotional side. My feelings could go from happy to sad and back to happy in the course of about ten minutes. I am still a little dramatic as an adult. But one thing my mom always did is validate my feelings. I didn't always express them in the right way, and sometimes I was downright wrong. But my mom didn't condemn me— she simply met me at the point of my pain or frustration and affirmed me. As a result, I felt understood.*

We parents won't always understand the feelings of our children, but we can validate that what they are feeling is real. Often the emotions of a young person are simply an outpouring of their personal experience and their internal world. Feelings represent *their reality*, and when we seek to understand that reality, we build a bridge of communication. *When we affirm the feelings of our young people we give them a sense of authenticity.* Affirming their feelings tells them they're cherished individuals with valid feelings. And when we identify with their excitement or disappointment, we let them know that we care and that they're understood for who they really are. Affirming your children's feelings is one of the most effective ways to identify with them, giving them a sense of being known and accepted.

5. Appreciate Your Child

Being the first child in a family and getting all the attention from your grandparents is really great. At least that is what little Scottie James, our grandson, thought until his little baby sister, Shauna, showed up.

Living close to our son, Sean, has allowed me (Dottie) to visit my grandson Scottie quite a bit. And when his sister was born I was doubly glad I lived nearby. Shauna was a delicate newborn, and three-year-old Scottie was a bit aggressive with his hugs of affection. Rather than scolding him when he gave his "attack hugs" to his sister I would step in and help him tone it down a little. I would guide him in gently stroking baby Shauna's head or hand. And as he did I would be effusive in my praise. "Wow, Scottie," I would say. "Grammy is so-o-o proud of how gentle you are with your baby sister!" Immediately Scottie's eyes would brighten and he would smile and nod his little head as if to say, "Thanks, Grammy, I needed that."

While acceptance is the foundation for a secure relationship, appreciation can be considered a cornerstone. *When we express appreciation to our kids, we give them a sense of significance,* the feeling or thought that they've done or said something worthwhile. Accepting young people tells them that their *being* matters; expressing appreciation to them says that their *doing* matters. Catch your kids doing something right and show appreciation. The more we caught our three daughters and son doing things right and expressed appreciation, the less likely there was an opportunity to catch them doing something wrong.

6. Show Affection to Your Child

What a way to start out—enveloped by the warm human touch of a mother for nine full months. There was never a moment you didn't feel connected and close as you grew in your mother's womb. And then after birth you probably felt the warm embrace of a mother's arms. From that time forward you and your children have had the need for affection.

Expressing affection to our kids through loving words and appropriate touch communicates that they're worth loving. *When we show affection to young people, we give them a sense of lovability.* Every expression of care and closeness provides emotional reinforcement, helping kids to realize they're loved. Affection can be expressed through words and appropriate physical contact.

We can say "I love you" to our children in a variety of different ways—a hug, a peck on the cheek, an arm around the shoulder, and so on. Words of affection or touching somehow reconnect us with one another and make us feel close. Perhaps nothing brings down defenses and allows us to open up to another than appropriate affection. No wonder Scripture instructs us to "greet one another with [affection] a holy kiss" (Romans 16:16 NIV).

7. Hold Your Child Accountable

I'm Sean, the only son in the McDowell family. I too appreciate how Mom and Dad built lasting relationships with us through acceptance, affirmation, availability, appreciation, and affection. But I also am glad they held us accountable.

I remember when I was in grade school and I really blew it. There were a couple of guys on the soccer team who didn't like me. I don't know why it was, but they pretty much ignored me and I felt left out. During class one day, our teacher, Mrs. Carlson, was getting after my two "not-so-close friends."

When she turned around to write something on the board, I had the idea to stand up for my teammates. I thought that might get me noticed and endear me to them. So I gave Mrs. Carlson a one-finger salute. Well, that got me noticed all right.

Right after class, all the kids, including my two teammates, gathered around me and treated me like a celebrity. Problem was, word got back to my mom and dad. And I immediately lost the celebrity status.

My parents didn't ground me, deny me a meal or two, or make me go to my room. They sat me down and calmly probed to figure out what I did and why I did it. They both led me to see how disrespectful my actions were to my teacher.

Acknowledging my wrong wasn't such a big deal. But what they said I needed to do was. They told me I needed to apologize to Mrs. Carlson in front of the entire class and also apologize to the class. My dad told me he would go with me if I wanted him to. I said I could do it on my own. It was a humiliating experience. But I learned I was responsible for my actions.

And there was a bonus. My soccer teammates thought my apology was the gutsiest thing they had ever seen. They became my friends after that.

To connect relationally with our kids we need to show them affirmation, acceptance, appreciation, affection, availability, and a sincere enthusiasm to approach their world. Still, if we don't balance these relational building blocks with loving limits and boundaries, they won't learn responsibility. *When we provide loving accountability to our young people, we give them a sense of responsibility.*

Accountability provides the parameters within which a young person can operate safely and securely. Kids need the loving authority of parents and other caring adults so they can learn to make responsible, right choices.

Relationships Make a Difference

None of us learn to make right moral choices in a vacuum. God intended that children learn to distinguish right from wrong and good from evil within the context of loving relationships. Simply warning your kids to avoid premarital sex isn't enough. The better your relationship, the better your warnings and teaching will stick. The rest of this book includes various tips and ideas for your conversations about the vital subject of sex. We encourage you to share them within the context of a loving relationship demonstrated by the 7 A's.

Part Two

Tips and Ideas for Your Conversations

Chapter 6

Who or What Most Influences Your Child's Behavior?

Thanks to the social-media revolution some of the most perverted and distorted views of sex are reaching our kids. They are just one click away, as we documented in chapter 1. Your kids are told that everyone is doing it. For the most part TV and the movies portray immorality as fun with no negative consequences. With the accessibility social and traditional media have to your kids, it's natural to think that they are the number-one influence on how your child acts.

Or perhaps it is your kids' friends who have the greatest influence on their behavior. Peer pressure is a powerful force. Maybe it is their heroes like Taylor Swift or perhaps Zac Efron, or film stars, musicians, celebrities, or athletes who sway the greatest influence.

This may surprise you, but a national online study showed that 45 percent of young people consider their parents to be their role models. Shattering stereotypes that parents and society hold about teens, the survey also revealed that only 32 percent looked to their friends and just 15 percent took inspiration from celebrities.[1] In fact, up until a child is 25 years old, studies show that the greatest influence on their behavior is a loving, close relationship with their father.[2] This doesn't de-emphasize the importance of mothers; it simply illustrates the powerful impact of the father.

Dr. Jean-Yves Frappier, a researcher at the University of Montreal's affiliated CHU Sainte-Justine Hospital Research Centre says, "Parents seem to underestimate their role and the impact that they have on their children."[3]

But here is the sad reality—studies show that "fewer than 15 percent of parents discuss sexuality with their children."[4] Yet teens say "they still trust their parents for the most reliable and complete information on sex."[5] Even with children trusting their parents more than anyone else—including teachers, pastors, or peers—the research still shows that "most parents have abdicated their responsibility. Instead, peers and the media have been the primary sources of sexuality information for America's children since the 1940s."[6]

Nonetheless, researchers at the University of Florida declare that, "The good news is that most teens ARE listening to what their parents are saying despite what we think!"[7]

One truth is obvious: *Teens listen to their parents.* At times it may not seem like it, but your kids are watching and listening. The research shows that "the number one reason teens give for abstaining from sex is their parents' disapproval."[8] Knowing this about your kids, it seems quite obvious you should be the first and primary source of information about sex for your child.

Well-known pastor Mark Driscoll and his wife, Grace, make a profound statement: "A child's sex education often comes through schools or churches. But a Christian parent should always be the first person to speak with their child about sex-related issues."[9] Home is where our kids should be learning about sex. Scripture works from that assumption. "Hear, my son, your father's instructions, and do not forsake your mother's teaching" (Proverbs 1:8 NASB). It is clear that *God wants Christian parents to be the primary sex educators of their children.*

You as a parent have a wonderful, God-given responsibility to instruct your children. And your children desperately need you. Attitudes, opinions, values, and instruction about sex can be one of the greatest gifts you can provide your children.

Young people should not grow up in programs...they should grow up in families. Before a child ever hears about sex from a "program," he/she should hear from mom and dad. And remember, whether you talk with your children about sex or not, others *are* talking—right now.

Chapter 7

Who Do Kids Want to Learn About Sex From?

You might think that sex would be a sensitive and even an embarrassing subject for children...so they would naturally be more comfortable learning about it from people other than their parents. But not so.

The Kaiser Foundation reports that

> *medical research and public health data tell us that when young children want information, advice, and guidance, they turn to their parents first. Once they reach the teenage years, they tend to depend more on friends, the media and other outsiders for their information.*[1]

The National Campaign to Prevent Teen Pregnancy's research concluded "that teens would like more guidance, information and conversation with parents and other adults about their early relationships."[2]

The encouraging news is that if you as a parent build a loving, warm relationship with your children early on, then in their teen years your kids will more likely depend more on you than on their friends, the media, and the Internet for information on sex. The Talk Institute observes that "most young people prefer that their parents be the primary source of sex information and that their mothers and fathers share equally in this responsibility."[3]

An American demographic study shows that "67 percent of teens 'give Mom an A.' They tell interviewers for the National Campaign to Prevent Teen Pregnancy that they want more advice about sex from their parents."[4] Recently ABC News reported that "young adolescents place parents at the top of their list of influences when it comes to their sexual attitudes and behaviors."[5] Your kids prefer you as their source of learning about sex. God has given you the privilege and opportunity to mold your child's sexual worldview.

Chapter 8

Why Do I Need to Talk to My Kids About Sex?

Sooner or later your child will learn the details about his or her sexuality. The issue isn't whether your child is going to learn it—the issue is in what context is he or she going to learn it. You have the opportunity to provide your child a healthy and proper understanding of sex or he or she will most likely be exposed to a perverted perspective of sex.

The Center for Effective Parenting concluded that

> *parents who avoid discussing the topic of sex with their children are doing their children a disservice. Such children may get the idea that sex is bad, which can affect them throughout their lives. Such children may seek information elsewhere, and this information can be incomplete or erroneous.*[1]

Authors Robert Crooks and Karla Baur point out that when parents become actively involved in their children's sex education, they "minimize some of the pitfalls faced by children and adolescents who turn to their peers for sex (mis)information."[2] And the truth is kids who feel their parents speak openly about sex and listen to them carefully are less likely to engage in high-risk behaviors. So it really comes down to your kids getting the right *information* about sex from you or *misinformation* from others.

But whether you are actually talking to your kids about sex you are still teaching them much about it. Whether you use words or not, your body language, attitude, relationships, the way you treat others, your comments about your children's friends, what you watch on TV, and what you "click on" at your computer—all of these things are teaching your children about sex.

Youth specialist Maggi Ruth Boyer nailed it when she said,

> *You communicate with your daughters and sons all the time about relationships and sexuality, simply by the way you live your life—by the way you treat, appreciate, and touch others. So, communication is happening, even if verbal conversations are not. Don't underestimate the power of your facial expressions and your expressions of affection.*[3]

Even if you don't talk consistently with your children about sex, they will still "hear" you because your body language and behavior will be speaking louder than your actual words.

I (Josh) recently had a conversation with Paul Roberts, who has worked with the Toronto branch of Youth for Christ for 40 years. He told me that most young people know far more about sex than their parents realize. Talking about sex is part of their world and is much more common and "out there" than a generation ago. Paul related that kids are often more comfortable with the topic than the parents trying to speak to them.

So often, parents will say, "It is so hard to talk to my child about sex." My immediate response is, "You think that is hard? Believe me, it's nothing compared to the conversation, 'Mom, I'm pregnant,' or

'I've got HPV.' Now *that* is a hard conversation!" If you don't have those tough talks with your children while they are younger, you will probably face much tougher talks later.

Chapter 9

Doesn't Talking About It Encourage It?

It may be natural to fear that if you talk with your kids about sexuality, they will go out and experiment with sex. Yet research and our own experiences prove otherwise.

Recent studies show that "adolescents who are well informed and comfortable in talking about sexuality with their parents are most likely to postpone intercourse."[1] *The Journal of Adolescence* reinforces this same conclusion: "Youths whose parents talked to them about right and wrong with regard to sexual behavior were significantly more likely to be abstinent than peers whose parents did not."[2]

Many parents think that talking about sex encourages it, yet "withholding information until you think your child is 'ready' can increase the chance that children will explore more on their own, go to others with less knowledge or different values than you, or accept inaccurate information as fact."[3]

Research done by the Campaign for Our Children found that "when parents teach their kids the facts about sex, their kids are

• less likely to have sexual intercourse as a teen;

- less likely to become pregnant or get someone pregnant as a teen;
- more likely to talk to parents about important issues in his or her life."[4]

Commit very early on to always be honest, loving, and open with your child about God's wonderful gift of sexuality. You won't be encouraging sexual promiscuity—you will be helping to discourage it.

Chapter 10

When Is the "Age-Appropriate" Time to Talk About Sex?

When should you start talking to your child about sex? You might fear that if you start too young it will be "too much, too soon." On the other hand, you may fear that if you don't deal with it, then later it might be "too little, too late." So what is the appropriate age to talk with your children about sex?

Adolescent medical professional Dr. Margaret Stager puts it this way:

> *Because of the society we live in, the consequences of avoiding these conversations far outweigh the consequences of giving too much information too soon, which is a rare circumstance. A bigger danger is that your children don't know your position, expectations or values...Parents can't control the flow of information between children at school or on the playground—kids are going to talk about sexuality. But you can't rely on schoolyard conversations or even school-sponsored classes to educate your child about sex.*[1]

So with that said, the problem is almost never "too much too soon," but rather "too little too late." A parent–child study found that "more than 40 percent of adolescents had had intercourse *before* talking to their parents about safe sex."[2]

In today's culture our kids are discovering sex and sexual behavior younger and younger, and you will want to be there first to introduce sex within the proper context. You don't have to rush your child into sexual education, but there's really no way of knowing how much your child knows or doesn't know without talking to them first.

Dr. Laura Rocker, child and adolescent psychiatrist for Akron Children's Hospital, suggests that sex education should "begin at birth. Children should learn the right words for their genitals along with other parts of their bodies. If you can be comfortable talking about it, this sets the tone for future discussions as the topic comes up."[3] You don't need to elaborate with more details than your child needs to answer his or her question. You will know when more information is needed, because they will probably ask.

Ignorance is dangerous and can be so destructive. Yet knowledge, combined with a loving relationship with one's parents, is the overriding factor leading to your child understanding that sex is God's design.

A very simple rule of thumb is that if you talk with your children when they are young, they will be comfortable to talk with you when they are older. The opposite is also true. Educator and speaker Sue Simonson puts it this way: "If we are not answering their questions at 2 and 3, they will not be asking them at 12 and 13."[4] If you wait to discuss sex with your kids until they are in their teens, they are undoubtedly going to be uncomfortable.

Joyce Kilmer, a parent educator in Washington, shares that her "best suggestion is to talk to kids really early, when they're too young to be embarrassed…It's less embarrassing for you, too, and they are very matter-of-fact at ages 4, 5 and 6. After they've been on the playground for a few years, and heard a lot of snickering, it's too late."[5]

When you are honest and tackle the topic of sex at the appropriate maturity levels of your kids—*you* become the expert to them! As they grow, they will trust you and listen to you. You will never be your child's only "sex educator," but you can (and should be) the first, primary, and most important sex educator in their lives.

Our daughter Katie, a mother of preschoolers, acknowledges from her own experience that "the earlier you start talking about it openly and simply, the easier it will be later when your children have important questions."

Heather (our baby—now a 26-year-old) remarked, "My earliest memory of my parents talking to me about sex is a little hard to distinguish, because unlike most parents that sit down and give you the whole sex talk in one uncomfortable exchange, it was pretty much dinner table conversation with our family from the time I was very young."

Maturity-Appropriate Rather than Age-Appropriate

Younger siblings need more straightforward answers and will need to be talked to earlier about sex than their older siblings. Why? The younger siblings are exposed to sexual and other issues faster because they receive earlier exposure. Your younger children grow up so much faster due to the fact they are listening to their older siblings and friends and then hearing you as a parent talk about the issues with their older siblings. So the appropriate time to discuss things is based more on their exposure level to information rather than a specific age.

As the mom and dad you need to follow your instincts. You

know your child better than anyone. I (Josh) found I needed to listen carefully to Dottie for wisdom about relating to the kids. We would interact about the maturity of each one of our children and what they needed to know and when they needed to know it. Dottie helped me to be open, honest, and sensitive. There is no set age that you share certain things with your children. The key, however, is to continually take advantage of the daily opportunities that arise.

Talk about sex in a way you feel comfortable. Each child is different. Remember, children don't need all the details at one time. Accurate information needs to unfold over a period of time. Each brief conversation lays the foundation for the next one. With each conversation you take it a step further in your child's proper understanding of his or her sexuality.

Here are two ideas to remember:

1. Few people overload a child with "too much too soon," but the problem usually is with "too little too late."

2. You need to be franker or give more honest answers than most parents think. For example, a three-year-old is a literalist. They may respond to "A baby is growing in mommy's tummy" with "Why did mommy eat the baby?" The child's only concept is that there is a "baby mixed with food in mommy's tummy." At this point a child needs just a simple response with a truthful answer.

The "Keeping Kids Healthy" syndicated program gives an excellent and realistic synopsis of how kids think:

Kids 2 through 5:

• Be aware that children of this age tend to be curious about the body and may wonder where babies come from.

- Remember that they require short answers. There's no need to give lots of information, which may only confuse kids too young to understand.

- Use correct names of body parts.

- Give value to your kids' questions.

- Always ask if they have any more questions.[6]

Kids 5 through 8:

- With children of this age, a parent can describe things very briefly: "When two grown-ups are married, love each other, and are committed to each other, it feels good when they hold and kiss each other, and one thing that feels good is for the husband to put his penis in the wife's vagina." The response may be "Yuck!" and the child may leave, but that's okay for now. Let them go.

- It's important to ask them whether they have any more questions.

Marriage and family counselor Dr. Corey Allen says: Talk about sex in a way that fits the age and stage of your child. A four-year-old doesn't need to know every detail of the sexual acts, but you can lay a solid foundation for later...For the most part, information they don't understand will roll off and be understood in a later conversation. Again, you don't have to go into every detail, but be prepared to later."[7] And be relaxed. Your body language speaks volumes. Your child will instinctively know if you are confident and comfortable. If you are he or she will come back to you again and again.

Remember, no matter what age your child is, it is never too late to start talking to them about God's wonderful gift of our sexuality. By starting with them when they are young you can build a trusting relationship that will pay off when they are older.

Chapter 11

Do I Start with the "Big Talk"?

She tapped me on the shoulder. "Mr. McDowell, thank you so much for what you shared. I have never heard anything like this before."

I had just finished a seminar talk on the "Bare Facts About Sex" and this mother wanted to let me know she was going to "apply" the message. She went on to say, "I've got to have my husband give our son 'the talk.'"

Without trying to sound alarmed, I replied, "How old is your son?" She said, "Thirteen." I had to control my surprise and astonishment. "You haven't been interacting with your son before this about sexual issues?" I asked. She said, "Oh, no…we haven't had the chance."

The "big talk" is a relic of the past, and never should have been endorsed in the first place! The *Journal of Family Issues* reported that "just half of adolescents feel they had one 'good talk' about sexuality during the past year with their mothers—and only one third with their fathers."[1]

Sexual issues are not learned in a "big talk." It is, instead, an unfolding process with information given out in little chunks at a time. Deal with issues and opportunities as they arise. Most young children cannot absorb or grasp more than just short conversations. They can and will forget the "big talk" very quickly.

The best sex education is 30 seconds here, 1 minute there, 10 seconds here, 2 minutes and 45 seconds there, and so on, starting as young as possible. When something comes up—step in, address it, and step back. Don't make a big deal out of it. In our family, about half of all conversations we had with our children about sex were no more than about two minutes each time.

For most children, the topic of sex comes in stages. They very seldom open up all at once. Kids open up as the result of an ongoing dialogue as they mature and grow older. Be ready, though, because when they do open up, it can often happen at the most inopportune times and places.

"For the life of me," says our son, Sean, "I cannot remember a first distinct time when I talked about sex with my parents. And I think that's because in my family, it was just a natural part of life. It's not that we talked about it all the time—but when it came up at the dinner table or in the car or before bed we simply talked about it. It was just like other topics—just a normal part of our conversation. So there was no one distinct time where I got the 'big talk.'"

Deb Koster of FamilyFire.com summed up a healthy approach:

> *In our family, we've always tried to have these conversations with our kids in simple and relaxed ways at young ages so the pressure for the "BIG TALK" never had a chance to build up. That way we created an environment where they felt comfortable coming to us with questions and we could be their source of information.*[2]

The Bible is clear about the most effective way to teach truth to our children. "Impress them on your children. Talk about them when you sit at home and when you walk along the road, when you lie down and when you get up" (Deuteronomy 6:7 NIV). Even the National PTA encourages this scriptural model: "Since most young children can only take in small bits of information at any one time, they won't learn all they need to know about a particular topic from a single discussion."[3]

The "Guide to Healthy Adolescent Development" from the Johns Hopkins Bloomberg School of Public Health offers these basic guidelines:

1. Have ongoing conversations with your children.

2. Share with small children slowly and in small chunks.

3. Do not try to cover all aspects of a question. For example, with the question "Mommy, how do babies come out?" all they need are short, simple (but honest), and accurate answers, such as "The baby comes out through a passage in mommy's body called a vagina."

4. As kids get older, they can handle more details and frankness.

5. Public questions often require (soft) public answers. For example: "You're in a crowded café, enjoying a salad with your eight-year-old, when suddenly she loudly asks, 'Mum, what's oral sex?' leaving you to wonder which is redder, you or the beetroot."[4]

In a situation like that you don't simply say, "Shut up and eat your salad." First try not to panic or act too surprised. But don't shy away from the question either. Instead, either answer it right away or calmly say, "Honey, let Daddy/Mommy answer that question as soon as we finish eating." Then, make sure you do answer.

One of the things I (Dottie) share with young mothers, including my own daughters, is this: You would never consider waiting to talk to your children about your faith in only "one big talk." You would lovingly and intentionally be sharing things about the Bible and God over time. It is similar regarding sex. We shouldn't assume that "one big talk" will answer every question our children have about the subject. Sex is a subject that must be examined early, often and with great patience, wisdom, loving-kindness and, at times, with a sense of humor. Relax and remember the key words: *early, often*, and *honestly*.

Chapter 12

What Can Happen If I Don't Talk to My Kids About Sex?

Pure and simple, if you don't talk to your kids about sex, someone else will. Your kids will gain an understanding about sex one way or another. And if you don't give them the right information, they will no doubt get misinformation. And that misinformation can range from the unfortunate to the tragic.

Author and pastor Jack Wellman shares his story.

> *I never knew my father. I lived with my aunt for a long time and no one ever talked about sex, so we learned about it from my friends and from the playground (or the street).*
>
> *It seemed that what I learned was always wrong too. I remember being told in the first grade that if I kissed a girl she would have a baby...needless to say I was terrified for a long time to even touch a girl, not to mention kiss one. When my aunt would kiss me, it horrified me because I didn't understand.*
>
> *So if you don't talk to your kids about sex, without embarrassment and without putting them off, they will learn about it one way or another. It will usually be wrong. There is never a*

question that your children should be afraid or embarrassed
to ask you. That kind of safe-zone builds trust and provides
an environment where they can come to you about anything.
And that is the best of situations; especially when they come to
the issue of sex.[1]

You have the opportunity to place sex within the context of a loving family and avoid the confusion and misinformation Jack experienced. But not talking to your kids about sex means they will learn it from other sources. And if that source is the Internet, that opens them up to the over 5 million pornographic websites that are out there.

As we mentioned in the first chapter of this book, when a child or teenager learns about sex from pornographic sites they learn about the misuse of sex—a distorted view of morality. But it also opens them up to becoming addicted to pornography.

Tragically, some parents are in denial and question if pornography is really harmful or that accessible. They ask, "What harm can it do?" Recently, a Christian tweeted me (Josh) in response to these warnings and said, "What does it matter what our kids see… our Gospel of Christ is compelling…why do you fear the Internet?"

Many studies have documented the adverse effects pornography has on an individual. In 2005, Dr. Jill Manning, author of *What's the Big Deal About Pornography?* testified before a U.S. Senate subcommittee on the harms of pornography. There she cited numerous effects that have been documented on children and adolescents when directly exposed to pornography. Some of the effects include

- lasting negative or traumatic emotional responses

- earlier onset of first sexual involvement

- increased risk for developing sexual compulsion and addictive behavior

- increased risk of gaining an incorrect and out-of-context view of sex
- the objectification of another human being for selfish sexual gratification[2]

Granted, all these negative effects may not be caused by casual or intermittent exposure to pornography. However, the real danger is in the massive amount of sexually perverted material that is available to your children. The sheer overexposure tends to desensitize a young person. Rather than gaining a correct biblical view of sexual morality, young people will tend to think everyone is doing whatever they want sexually. This is clearly the impression given through cyberspace.

We will not be able to protect our children from all the misinformation or perverted views about sex they may hear about or see. But if we are the ones who reach our kids first with God's design for sex, it will go a long way in insulating them from the negative impact of pornography, perverted morality, and the misinformation about sex.

Chapter 13

What If My Kids Are Too Curious About Sex?

Children by nature are curious—some more than others. And there is something fascinating, mysterious, and intriguing about sex that makes all of us curious. So the issue isn't with our kids being too curious. The problem occurs when their curiosity isn't satisfied.

It is completely normal and natural for our kids to wonder about sex and want to have answers to their questions. There is a real danger if we don't respond to their curiosity. Remember, they will get answers from somewhere or someone. The National Physicians Center for Family Resources states that "curiosity about sex will not go away if it is never discussed. In fact, avoiding the subject can make sex seem even more mysterious and exciting."[1]

Recent studies have shown that "before age 10, children usually are not sexually active or preoccupied with sexual thoughts, but they are curious and may start to collect information and form myths about sex from friends, schoolmates, and family members."[2]

How a child's curiosity is satisfied from 4 to 12 years of age often determines their sexuality from 12 to 18 years old. Drs. Clea McNeely and Jayne Blanchard of Johns Hopkins Bloomberg School of Public Health explain:

It is by far best for a child to get his or her curiosity satis-
fied by mom and dad. Their curiosity at this age is criti-
cal because their sexual attitudes during their teen years are
often formed by the answers they get to their curiosity before
10 years old (6 to 10 years).[3]

What a privilege and opportunity to mold our children's lives and their future behavior. Answering honestly is their best guide. The general rule in the McDowell household was to give a brief, simple, accurate answer…just enough to satisfy their curiosity—for example, "Girls have vulvas and vaginas, and boys have penises and testicles." They don't need a lengthy, in-depth, Sex 101 answer. Much more than a short answer will often bore a child.

When our children were young they were curious about their private parts. When I (Dottie) would bathe them, I would routinely refer to body parts with their correct descriptions. I made it a point to talk about private parts as calmly and deliberately as I did fingers, toes, and ankles. This was an intentional decision to communicate a natural comfort level when discussing our bodies. This honesty early on set the stage for relaxed discussions later.

A preschooler is content with vague sexual information such as "Babies grow inside mommies." But later on, there will be questions and curiosity about how the baby gets inside the mom's tummy. They may ask questions like "Does Mommy vomit up the baby?" Or "Does Daddy unzip Mommy's tummy?" Or "Does Mommy poop the baby out?" The child is looking for simple, honest explanations.

Parenting specialist Margaret Renkl gives an excellent answer: "'Most babies come out through the mommy's vagina.' If your child asks a follow-up question, then you can add, 'The vagina is like a tube inside the mommy. It stretches really wide so the baby can get outside.'"[4]

No matter what the age, our children deserve honest answers, but those answers need to be scaled down to their level of maturity. And just because a teen or pre-teen has questions about how a girl gets pregnant, what condoms are for, or what oral sex is, that doesn't mean they are planning to become sexually active. It's best to answer their questions without assuming that curiosity is a danger sign. The danger sign is in not satisfying their curiosity with honest answers.

Chapter 14

What About Using "Nicknames" for Body Parts?

Her face was red and her voice reflected anything but calm. "I think it is absolutely disgusting that you told your son, 'It's your penis.' I told my son it was his 'ding-dong.'"

This pastor's wife took issue with me (Josh) during a break at one of my seminars on the "Bare Facts About Sex." I calmly explained to her that "an ear is called an ear, a nose is called a nose, an eye is called an eye, a vagina is called a vagina, and a penis is called a penis." I didn't figure it was my place to rename body parts. Obviously this lady disagreed.

Children will often explore their body parts. And when they reach a certain age they will often ask questions. When talking to them or answering their question, be honest and answer with correct anatomical names of their body parts.

We always wanted to refer to our children's sexual organs as their "private parts" with an emphasis on "private." It's part of sending the message that they are "private parts" and are to remain private.

When talking with a child, it's best to refer to their private parts early with correct words: a penis is a penis, not your "willy" or your "ding-dong." It's not your "down there" or "that place" either.

When you use correct words like *penis, testicles, vulva,* or *vagina,* explain not only what they are but also what they do. Your kids will find out sooner or later, and it's becoming much sooner now because of the Internet. And you will want to become your child's authority on what body parts he or she has and what they are called. You don't want it to be the Internet.

I (Josh) was playing with one of our daughters, who at the time was about three years old. Dottie walked into the room and our daughter blurted out, "Mommy, Daddy touched my vagina!" Dottie tried not to look alarmed. I took a deep breath and responded in a very calm but deliberate voice and asked our daughter, "Honey, where is your vagina?" She smiled and touched her belly button. Then I proceeded to explain in the simplest language I could the difference between her vagina and her belly button.

It may take a number of little discussions and explanations for a child to get the body parts figured out. But by using their correct names and explaining what they're for, your child won't be embarrassed or shamed when they find out the real names of their body parts.

Chapter 15

How Much Knowledge Must I Have?

Knowing about the problem of easy access to the Internet and all forms of media in our homes and schools is only half the battle. We must also provide knowledge—*accurate* knowledge to responsibly and constructively teach our kids God's design and purpose for sex.

Wise King Solomon said,

> *It is not good to have zeal without knowledge, nor to be hasty and miss the way (Proverbs 19:2 NIV).*

It was interesting that while doing extensive research on talking with our kids about sex, almost *all* the studies reported that one of the top three things parents can do to help their children say "no" to sexual pressure is to not just share information or knowledge, but share *accurate* knowledge.

In *A Guide to Healthy Adolescent Development*, Clea McNeely and Jayne Blanchard wrote, "Research actually suggests that young people who are knowledgeable about sexuality and reproductive health are less likely to engage in early sexual activity." The researchers concluded that "providing accurate, objective information to adolescents supports healthy sexual development."[1]

An article in *Healthy Children Magazine* states, "Sharing factual information with and giving good moral guidance to your teenager is a vitally important part of helping your teen understand herself or himself. It can help your child avoid devastating, and possibly life-threatening, errors in judgment."[2]

A positive way a parent can significantly influence sexual behavior is to be a source of accurate information. A great source of accurate information for parents is the Medical Institute for Sexual Health (www.medinstitute.org). It may require a significant effort to accurately grasp the issues around our children's sexuality, but it will be worth it. The Internet presence of premarital sex demands that we be educated parents.

If our children find that we as parents are not honest and accurate, they will lose trust in us and we will lose influence. And count on it—our kids will often "Google" their questions on the Internet and compare the answers with the ones we give them.

But don't panic if you don't know an answer to a question. Don't be afraid to admit you don't know the answer. Suggest that you will find out and get back to them (and then make sure you do). Or suggest the two of you find the answer together. What a great time this can be of learning and bonding for both you and your child!

Admitting that you don't know an answer but you'll find it will cause your children to trust you even more. Then when you do share the answers to their questions, it will give you greater credibility.

The Issues

The following are just some of the issues about which we need to be knowledgeable. Parenting is a great adventure, but also a time consuming and demanding experience. There are not a lot of short-cuts.

- explanation of anatomy and reproduction in males and females including menstruation and nocturnal emission

- sexual intercourse and pregnancy

- fertility and birth control

- other forms of sexual behavior, including oral sex, masturbation, and petting

- sexual orientation, including heterosexuality, homosexuality, and bisexuality

- the physical and emotional aspects of sex, including the differences between males and females

- self-image and peer pressure

- sexually transmitted diseases

- rape and date rape, including how being intoxicated (drunk or high) or accepting rides or going to private places with strangers or acquaintances puts you at risk

- how choice of clothing and the way you present yourself sends messages to others about your interest in sexual behavior

- condoms

- emotions

- God's definition of true love

- flirtation

- what the Bible has to say about these issues

Parenting specialists Kristin Zolten and Dr. Nicholas Long, writing for the Center for Effective Parenting, explain that "you need to first educate yourself about sex education. The more parents know about various sex topics, the more comfortable they will be answering their children's questions. This knowledge should include information about all aspects of sex, including reproduction, sexual organs, birth control, sexually transmitted diseases, and so on."[3]

We don't have to know it all, but we do need to be ready and willing to have enough accurate knowledge and information to answer our kids' questions.

Chapter 16

Shouldn't Certain Issues Be Off-Limits?

Some of the material our kids are seeing and reading is horrific. Much of it is shocking and makes us uncomfortable. Yet from the moment our children are born, we need to create an atmosphere of openness and approachability that makes any and all questions from them acceptable. If you act repulsed or surprised or appear uncomfortable about your child's question, it may be the last question he or she will ask. No question should be off-limits.

The attitude that no questions are taboo will have a tremendous impact on your child's understanding and behavior. But you need to verbalize your openness. Jerald Newberry, Executive Director of the National Education Association's Health Information Network says, "You want to be someone the child feels comfortable in coming to with questions. Let your children and teens know that you are always open to discussing anything."[1]

As we've mentioned before, after verbalizing that "no question is off-limits," you then need to demonstrate it in your attitude and body language. "Treat the topic of sex matter-of-factly," says Dr. Nicholas Long of the Center for Effective Parenting. He continues,

When discussing sex with their children, parents should try to treat these discussions as they would any other important

topic—calmly and matter-of-factly. Children are very per-
ceptive, and they will be able to tell if their parents are
uncomfortable with the topic of sex. If children sense that
their parents are uncomfortable with the topic of sex, they
will be less likely to come to their parents with problems and
questions later on. Children might also be led to believe that
sex is bad or wrong, or a taboo subject.[2]

Whenever I (Dottie) would be talking with one of the children about sexual matters I always wanted to be calm. If I was comfortable about it, I sensed they were comfortable. I tried to talk about it with the same tone in my voice that I would use if I were talking about what's for dinner, how much a haircut costs, or where the dog's collar was at. In other words, if my kids sensed that I was as relaxed with this subject as I was with any other, they were less hesitant to come to me with their questions or concerns about sex.

But what if you can't answer the question? There is always an answer, even if it's "I don't know, but let's find out." The important thing is how you respond. When you can convey the message that no subject is off-limits you are on your way to effectively talking to your kids about sex.

Pastor Jack Wellman strongly admonishes that "there is never a question that your children should be afraid or embarrassed to ask you. Tell them that. That safe-zone builds trust and provides an environment where they can come to you about anything. And that is the best of situations; especially when they come to you about sex."[3]

Heather, our youngest married daughter, recently told us, "Sex was dinner-table conversation—there wasn't really anything that I felt uncomfortable asking. I knew that if I wanted to know something, I could ask you guys and you would tell me. I don't remember anything being really 'off the table' and I don't think anything is still off the table."

We are thankful that message got through to our kids. Be open, honest, and willing to find answers to any question your child has no matter what it is, and you won't regret it.

Chapter 17

How Often Should I Talk to My Kids About Sex?

Should I converse about sex with my kids once a quarter, once a month, bimonthly, or weekly? Well, it's not about how many talks you have, the important thing is that you say many of the same things over and over and over again. Repetition is part of the process.

Many children cannot take in more than two to three minutes of information at a time. Children Now, a children's health and education organization, states,

> Since most young children can only take in small bits of information at any one time, they won't learn all they need to know about a particular topic from a single discussion. That's why it's important to let a little time pass, then ask the child to tell you what she remembers about your conversation. This will help you correct any misconceptions and fill in missing facts.[1]

Don't be surprised when your four-year-old asks the same question she asked when she was three, or be surprised when the same is asked when she is five. You will feel like saying, "I've told you where babies come from before" or "I've explained to you a number of times what your belly button is."

I (Dottie) recently talked with Dr. Joe McIlhaney, chairman of the Medical Institute for Sexual Health. He pointed out that parents often feel they talk to their kids about sex more than their kids feel they have actually been talked to about it. There is probably a good reason for that. Parents invest a lot of emotional energy in trying to be clear with enough, but not too much, information about the subject. And they tend to remember those moments. Yet for a child, he or she is simply listening. So those moments may not be that memorable. That is why we need to be patient and supportive and say it again and again and again.

The issue of sex has a lot of complexity. And it will take time for our children to understand it all. "Nashville mom Laura Hileman once heard her 3-year-old son explaining to his brother, 'Boys have penises, and girls have china.' And don't be surprised if the question comes up again and again while your little one sorts it all out."[2]

When we are patient and willing to explain it again (maybe with a few more details) it sends a strong message to a child.

Many studies show the following:

> *Repetition of sexual communication (as opposed to one-shot discussions) is likely to be important for several reasons. 1) Repetition may enhance an adolescent's understanding, processing, and acceptance of parental sexual messages; 2) it is likely to increase feelings of comfort regarding sexual conversation; 3) it conveys sincere parental interest to the adolescent; and 4) fosters a more connected parent-adolescent relationship, which in turn, has important implications for promoting adolescent sexual health.*[3]

Repetition is viewed differently by our children than by us as parents. They need the process of repetition to build their understanding and comprehension about sex one brick at a time. And that means we repeat the same concepts, perhaps a little differently or with fuller meaning, again and again and again.

Chapter 18

Won't They Think I'm Obsessed If I Keep Harping on the Sex Issue?

To harp—"to dwell on a subject tiresomely." No one likes to hear someone harping on any subject. And yes, if we as parents keep harping on the sex issue our kids will think we're obsessed and they may shut us out. Yet we need to get the truths about sex, especially God's design, purpose, and boundaries for sex, instilled within our children. So how do we do that?

Instead of harping, take advantage of real-life situations and translate them into *teachable moments*. A teachable moment is a situation or opportunity that opens the door to take advantage of an everyday circumstance to bring up the subject of sex. It might be a conversation with your child about a difficult subject, sensitive issue, sexuality itself, or anything else, but important enough to interact with your child right at that moment. These moments could be prompted by something he or she encountered on the computer, heard from a friend, saw on TV, a video, a poster, even something he or she read in a children's book. Seize these opportunities.

Capturing teachable moments is a learned "art." And the more media literate you are the better. This means you understand how to interpret and evaluate media content as it relates to values and behavior—the Internet, movies, TV, magazines, comics, newspapers, blogs, tweets, and other social media messages.

Today's culture provides every parent with a lot of media opportunities to translate into teachable moments. A Kaiser Family Foundation report on TV broadcasts shows that "75 percent of network prime-time shows contain either sexual dialogue or sexual behavior."[1]

The entertainment media, especially TV and the Internet, have become the primary sexual influences or educators in the world. It is so critical that we monitor the destructive content of the media. We can mitigate the impact by interacting with our children and turning it into something positive.

For example, during the 2012 Super Bowl halftime show, many were shocked and others were amused when M.I.A. flipped her middle finger at the camera. She showed a physical finger that has the sexual overtone of "F—— you!" How many Christians showed disgust with that (and appropriately so) but then missed a golden opportunity to impart an important truth about sexuality that would be remembered for years by a child? That was a teachable moment to take a negative and turn it into a positive.

I (Josh) was riding in our van with Kelly and Sean, then nine and seven. And like normal kids at that age they got into a dispute. Out of frustration, Sean shouted at his sister. "F—— you!" I could have been enraged and harshly disciplined my son. But in that situation, I didn't show any surprise or emotion. I simply asked, "Son, do you know what that means?" He immediately replied, "No." So I asked, "Where did you hear it?" He responded, "At school."

I said to Sean, "Son, can I explain to you what it means?" With his eyes as big as quarters, he said, "Yes."

The next ten minutes were a wonderful time of teaching and

sharing with my children. I explained what the phrase meant. I told them how it demeaned one of the most beautiful gifts of sex that God has ever given to daddies and mommies. Then I tried to be as clear as possible on a seven-to-nine-year-old level why, in our family, we don't use that word. That incident became an ideal teachable moment that had a positive impact on Sean's life.

The opportunities are unlimited to have very significant teachable moments with our children. These small moments, in any number of situations, can turn a negative into a positive memorable experience, and can literally influence the attitudes, beliefs, understanding, and behavior of our children.

The following are areas that often provide teachable moments in our daily life.

1. TV and other entertainment media. In *Sexuality, Contraception, and the Media,* the American Academy of Pediatrics reported that

> *American children devote more than 38 hours per week to various forms of media, such as television, videos, video games, music, and the Internet. By the time the average teen graduates from high school he or she will have squandered 15,000 hours watching television—that's twenty percent more time than the 12,000 hours he or she will have spent in the classroom. Furthermore, the average American adolescent will view nearly 14,000 sexual references per year.*[2]

The news is full of material for teachable moments. The "Wait for Sex" parent curriculum developed by the Resource Center for Adolescent Pregnancy Prevention provides this insight: "You and your child are watching the news on TV. The reporter talks about the family of a seventh grade girl filing a lawsuit against the school district for sexual harassment. A boy at the school has repeatedly made derogatory remarks about her body, especially her breasts. This is a great segue to talk about how important it is to show respect to the opposite sex."[3]

At times we would be watching a TV show or DVD with our kids and be blindsided when it depicted or hinted at two people having immoral sex. We would simply shut off the show and turn it into a teachable moment.

We would say, "Kids, what is wrong with what just happened?" Then they would talk and we would listen.

"Why is it wrong?"

We would listen without interrupting.

"What can be the consequences of nonmarital sex? Can you recall ever seeing negative consequences of sexual activity on TV or in a DVD?"

Usually, they couldn't, because the entertainment media almost never shows the negative consequences of nonmarital sex. For example, hardly anyone ever gets a sexually transmitted disease on TV. Of course that is totally unrealistic in the real world.

Today, one out of every four teenagers is infected with an STD. Three *million* young people will get an STD this year alone. Fifty percent of all men 12 to 70 years old are infected with HPV. There is no cure; condoms are inadequate; and it is killing more women every year than HIV.* But we rarely see it on TV or in the movies. It is both unrealistic and misleading—immoral actions do have consequences. The misconceptions presented by the media about sexual consequences provide us an ideal teachable moment with our kids.

Another approach to teachable moments is to put the entire

---

*For more details, see *The Bare Facts* book and DVD resources, described in the back pages of this book.

conversation in the light of God's Word and his purpose for sex. When you are watching TV or movies together, you see many story lines showing people making poor sexual choices. Discuss with your child why God gave us certain guidelines and boundaries on sex. Use this as a time to reinforce how Scripture is relevant and adherence to it is in our best interest.

The American Psychological Association also gives some excellent advice:

> *Speak up. If you don't like a TV show, CD, video, pair of jeans, or doll, say why. A conversation with her will be more effective than simply saying, "No, you can't buy it or you can't watch it." Support campaigns, companies, and products that promote positive images of girls. Complain to manufacturers, advertisers, television and movie producers, and retail stores when products sexualize girls.*[4]

A recent SIECUS report (Sexual Information & Education Council of the U.S.) had some good advice:

- Share your opinions and values in a positive way. Discuss your thoughts. Your children need to understand your values as they begin to form their own.

- Watch for teachable moments. Use the opportunity in a joke, song, billboard, or TV commercial to discuss a subject.

- Use commercial time to talk. Take this time to communicate your own brief message. Your children may pay more attention during a break in the show.

- Remember that "bad" shows can provoke discussion too. They will often give you the opportunity to discuss the behavior of a certain character.

• Be sensitive. Your children might find it embarrassing for you to discuss sexuality issues in front of their friends or other adults.[5]

Use the media to your advantage. Interact with your kids. Share *your* values.

2. A pregnant woman. Children are often intrigued by seeing a pregnant woman be it a stranger, a relative, or a family friend. This is a time you can answer their questions and easily transition into a conversation about sex.

3. Real stories about real people. Author Wendy Sellers points out how to take advantage of real stories. "Children respond to stories of real people. For example say, 'I feel sad about some news I just heard. My cousin's son has to drop out of school to get a job. He and his girlfriend had sex, and now she's pregnant. He will have to work and pay child support instead of finishing his education. What do you think about that?'"[6] These real stories provide excellent teachable moments.

Diana Converse, a family life educator at Hillsborough County University of Florida extension, provides the next six situations for teachable moments.

4. Nude pictures. "Your child and his playmate are giggling in the bedroom. You open the door to see what's so funny and find them both looking at a naked woman in the encyclopedia."[7] This is a powerful teachable moment.

5. Wanted posters. "As you are waiting in line at the post office with your 11-year-old son, you notice an FBI 'Wanted' poster on the wall. One of the men posted is wanted for the rape of three women."[8] What an opportunity to talk to your child!

6. Homosexual affection. "You and your child notice two men holding hands at the shopping mall."[9] Another teachable moment— to compassionately explain homosexuality.

7. Discovering a condom. "While doing the laundry, you find a condom in your son's pocket."[10] This can become a teachable moment—a rather shocking one, but a teachable moment all the same.

8. Sex misinformation. "While driving home from school one day, your 13-year-old daughter says, 'Mom, I heard you can't get pregnant the first time you have sex.'"[11]

9. Interfamily differences on sex. "Your mother-in-law is changing the diaper of your six-month-old son. You and your older son are watching her change the diaper. Your mother-in-law gently hits the baby's hand and tells the baby, 'Don't touch yourself down there.'"[12] You would probably want to hold off with an immediate response. But later you can use this situation as a positive teachable moment.

10. Look at family albums of weddings. What a wonderful teachable moment!

11. Animal behavior. One of the McDowell daughters shares this story: "I know my mom says that the first time we talked explicitly about sex was when we were driving down the road and I saw two cows with one climbing on top of the other. She said I asked what was going on. Mom explained it and I said, 'Oh, wouldn't that be gross if people did that?' And, of course, that became the first conversation we had about intercourse. The strange thing is, I have no memory of that conversation." While our daughter doesn't remember the situation, it was one of those teachable moments that, little by little, gave her enough information to understand God's wonderful gift of sex.

12. School assemblies, sporting events, practice, school plays, and so on. We were at a restaurant having dinner with all four of our children—Kelly, Sean, Katie, and Heather—when Sean said, "Dad, there was a speaker at school today who spoke on sex. We don't think that you would agree with him." I immediately replied, "Why?"

For the next three hours or so, we sat at that Stuart Anderson Steakhouse in Lakeside, California, and had an open family discussion. The waiter (a college student) kept hanging around us. Finally, he interrupted and said, "Kids, do you know how fortunate you are to have a mom and dad who will discuss these things with you? My parents never did that with my sister and me and as a result, we've made some very bad choices." Use these times as teachable moments.

13. Music. Researchers from the State University of New York at Albany released an analysis of song lyrics from the 174 songs that made it into the Top 10 country, pop, and R&B Billboard charts in 2009. They found that "92 percent contained one or more 'reproductive messages,' with an average of 10.49 such phrases per song."[13]

Years ago, I (Josh) walked into Sean's room while he was attempting to erase a song on his new Depeche Mode CD. He was 12 at the time.

"Sean, what in the world are you doing?" I inquired.

"I'm trying to erase a song."

"Why?"

"It doesn't meet our family standard, so I want to erase it."

This provided me a different type of teachable moment. Immediately, I expressed my admiration for him and how proud I was for the choice he had made.

Deb Roffman, writing for the PTA, reinforces this. She said, "When you see something that doesn't uphold those values (commercial, television show, music video) point it out to your child. Be your child's cultural interpreter."[14]

14. Bath time. When one of my daughters was about two years old, I had recently come home from a tour and Dottie asked me, "Would you please give her a bath?" I told her I would and went into our master bathroom and started filling the bathtub with water. I told my daughter, "Honey, now get undressed, but don't get in," because I was always afraid of my kids slipping and hitting their head. So I told her, "Wait till Daddy gets back. I've got a surprise for you!"

While I was traveling, I had gotten her a little rubber ducky, so I went to get it for her. Just as I was about to go back into the bathroom, she let out a piercing scream. I dashed back into the bathroom with my heart beating wildly, and exclaimed, "Honey, what's wrong?" My little girl was sitting on the edge of the bathtub looking at herself. She looked up at me and said, "Daddy, Daddy, my penis is inside out!"

You see, my daughter had seen her brother. What else would you think as a two-year-old? She had either lost her penis or it was inside out. That was a genuine concern for her.

This was a great teaching moment. "Oh, no, honey," I said. "That's how God made you. He makes little boys like your brother with a penis, and little girls like you with a vagina. Isn't that wonderful what God has done? Now, let's take our bath."

It was a 20-second conversation. It was great sex education. It was a teachable moment. As you take advantage of all the above situations and more that can lead to great conversations, remember that if you involve your children in teachable moments when they are young, they will interact with you on teachable moments when they are older.

Chapter 19

Just How Much Should I Monitor My Kids' World?

Monitoring your child's world is an absolute necessity in today's world if you expect to protect your kids. Your concern shouldn't be so much whether you're monitoring your kids too much, but if you're monitoring them too little.

What are the areas you need to monitor? Obviously, that would include your kids' friends and their families, their school, their athletic groups, the TV, the movies and the videos they watch, the magazines they read, the music they listen to and, of course, the Internet. This is a big order—but it must be done.

In today's world as a parent, we will have to be courageous and undaunted in monitoring our child's world. We are facing challenges (because of the Internet) that we never even dreamed about facing before. In fact, our daughter Katie (a mother of preschoolers) told me (Dottie) recently that she has "given up hope that she can protect her boys from the culture around them." Her strategy, then, was "not to *protect* them *from* it, but to *prepare* them *for* it, by understanding it, knowing how to deal with it, and helping her children to walk through it." This approach requires intentional, and sometimes hard, choices.

We can seek creative ways to dive into our kids' worlds. My (Dottie's) sister, the mother of a high-school daughter, is a great example of someone who found a creative solution. She is a certified teacher who wanted to be a stay-at-home mom, but also wanted to be able to be right in the middle of her daughter's world. To accomplish this goal, she subs at her daughter's school. This way she can get to know the kids her daughter hangs out with, meet the other teachers, and get a feel for the atmosphere in her daughter's school. Of course, not all of us can arrange such an ideal situation. However, we *all* can be creative and determined.

Josh and I were diligent about this and expected to have a clear dialogue with our kids about their comings and goings. We required that they tell us exactly where they were going, what time they would arrive and depart, what they were doing, and who they were with. This took time, energy, and determination. But it was important for their safety and for our peace of mind.

We established ground rules and curfews, and expected certain behavior. We included our kids in the process of making the rules so that they could understand our perspectives and concerns. We did all this within the context of a loving relationship, knowing that otherwise they may have resisted. Remember, "Rules without a relationship often lead to rebellion."

As our kids got older and reflected more and more signs of maturity and responsibility, we would ease up on the reins. This was a "process of preparation," knowing that eventually they would be headed to work or college on their own and would be making these choices alone. We did have to occasionally remind them that supervising and monitoring their whereabouts didn't make us nags—it made us parents!

When your child is playing at a neighbor's house, it's important to know who else will be there and that someone you trust (an adult) will be in charge. Sadly, abuse often comes from other children, so you need to know who will be in the home. Before your children go somewhere new, be assured that there is no pornography in that home. A young couple that lives near us always asks if there is an older brother in the family where their children have been invited. If there is, they have a family policy that the kids must play at their house, not at the neighbor's. They also have a policy that no teenage boy will ever babysit their kids. This may seem strict, but it is simply for the safety of their children.

Know what is being taught in your children's schools. Schools have very different policies, depending on what state you are in and whether the school is public or private. Get involved. Volunteer in the classroom. Go to PTA meetings and meet with the teachers. Keep your eyes on public policy and know what laws are being voted on that can affect your school district.

Monitor your kids' TV, movies, and DVD viewing. Each family needs to make policies that are in the best interest of their children. Two of our grown kids have chosen not to even have a TV in their homes. Another one of our kids carefully screens all TV programs. Be in touch with what movies and DVDs are out there, and have a plan that reflects your family's standards. Use discussions about these things as "opportunities." Kids need to understand that the media are overflowing with material that sends out the wrong messages. As much as possible read what your kids read and listen to what they listen to. You can then interact with them about the messages that flow out of the books and the songs they care about. This kind of monitoring gives you more opportunities to connect, more opportunities to understand and more opportunities to bond with your kids.

Wisdom from a 27-Year-Old's View of Children and the Internet

Today it is inevitable that our children will get on the Internet.[1] There is no way around it—the school systems even assign homework that can only be done on the web.

There are many different protection software platforms we can use. Some of these programs cost money and some do not. Some of the software programs work on smart devices and some do not. Software to consider:

X3 Watch—pay/free	www.x3watch.com/
Total Net Guard—pay	http://afo.net/
Bsecure—pay	www.bsecure.com/
Net Nanny—pay	www.netnanny.com/
Covenant Eyes—pay	http://covenanteyes.com/
K9 Web Protection—free	www1.k9webprotection.com/
Safe Eyes—free	www.internetsafety.com/
Cyber Sitter—pay	www.cybersitter.com/
Pure Sight—pay	www.puresight.com/

We need to be aware that filter software is not a perfect solution. The software will block most sites, but not all of them and not e-mail.

To protect my children I am taking the following steps:

1. All computers and smartphones are to be turned off no later than 9 p.m. There is a saying that "nothing good happens after 10 p.m."

2. I do not allow my children to keep computers, televisions, or smart devices in their rooms overnight.

3. I know their friends and their friends' parents. I'm not saying my children cannot have friends who are not believers, but I want those children to be at my home. I want to know that when my child goes to someone else's home, they have similar standards as I do.

4. I want my children to understand that being on the Internet is a privilege, not a right they automatically receive from birth. Call me old-fashioned or old-school, but I want my kids reading books and playing outside using their imagination.

5. I set a certain allotment of time my children can spend on the Internet. I saw one particular software company that allows parents to use time on the Internet as a reward system. They could accumulate minutes on the Internet by doing chores and helping out around the house. I like the idea of awarding 10 minutes for making the bed, 10 minutes for doing the dishes, 20 minutes for vacuuming the house, and so on.

6. I don't put any computers in my home in a nonpublic or secluded area.

7. I don't go to bed while my child is on a computer or smart device.

8. Finally, any rule that I make for my children, I follow myself. I want to be an example for my children to follow in all aspects of my life, including my respect and caution when it comes to the Internet and social media.

This mom may sound overprotective to some people. But if we are to err on one side or the other, we would suggest erring on the side of overprotection.

A Family Violated by Digital Porn

In January of 2012 the lives of Melissa, Tom, and their children changed forever.* The police showed up at their house to interview their oldest son, 13-year-old Kyle. Under questioning, Kyle admitted to being addicted to pornography and to have crossed sexual boundaries with two of his siblings and a little boy who visited their house often. Melissa and Tom were utterly shocked. Their son was taken from their house that day and put into juvenile detention. He was charged with three counts of sexual abuse, one of them a felony.

Melissa and Tom have raised their children in the admonition of the Lord. They have helped them know right from wrong, prayed for them, taught them, and protected them to the best of their ability. They would have never thought that any of their children would view pornography, let alone act on it. But they were naïve about its power and accessibility.

Kyle had been exposed to pornography and became addicted very fast. He had been sneaking into his parents' room and using their laptop, which didn't have any filter on it. He had also been viewing porn with his friends on their smartphones. He had friends come over often with their handhelds, and they had asked Melissa for the family's wi-fi password to "listen to Christian music." She'd ignorantly given it to them, not realizing that the phones kept the password and would automatically allow them access every time they came over. Kyle couldn't handle what he saw. He couldn't get the images out of his mind, and he acted on those images through sexual abuse.

At the age of 13 Kyle's life has been changed forever. After a period of house arrest at a relative's, he is now on probation

---

*Names and details have been changed to conceal the identity of those involved.

and is going through an intense two-year therapy program. Only recently was he allowed contact with one of his siblings. And he will not return to his home until after the program. His "juvenile sex offender" status will show up on all background checks for the rest of his life.

After Kyle was caught he wanted to share his story. He started insisting that Melissa and Tom warn his friends and their parents to stay far away from the path of pornography and addiction. His background of being raised knowing the love of Christ did not keep him from the pornography...but it has helped him deal with what has happened in his life since. He has been on his knees asking for redemption and praying that his story will make a difference.

Chapter 20

When Does Monitoring Become an Invasion of Privacy?

As a child grows, privacy becomes more and more important to them. Allowing a young person to have privacy demonstrates you trust and respect them. Yet that trust and respect must be earned.

One of the things we at the McDowell household did was establish a "no locked bedroom door policy" for the kids. As their parents, we could lock our bedroom door, for obvious reasons—but our kids could not lock theirs. Yet we did want to respect our children and their need for private time. Despite our curiosity about what our kids were doing in their rooms for hours with the door closed, we told our children that we would *always* knock before entering their room because we respected their privacy.

After we had stood in front of many a closed door, rapping with our knuckles and calling out before entering, our kids knew that we would always knock before entering. That policy resulted in our kids respecting and trusting us more. Child specialist Mary Van-Clay shares this:

> *If an environment of trust and respect has been established, and your child's privacy is respected, not only does that trust*

and respect grow, but your child has the opportunity to prac-
tice setting his or her own boundaries with whatever is con-
sidered private (for example, time, his or her body, his or her
room or space).[1]

But how do you handle your child's Facebook page? Should your child's e-mail be private too? Or should you have access to your child's text messages or e-mail? Our answer is, *Absolutely!* You should have access to all your child's social-networking sites. Your kid's room is not the same as their Facebook page. Facebook, e-mail—any of the social-media sites your child uses should be accessible by you. Monitoring your kid's activity online is not only within your parental rights and responsibility—it is your means to protect them.

However, much like the door to the room, rather than barging into your child's digital "space," consider negotiating with your son or daughter how you would have access to their networking sites. Rather than invading their space uninvited try negotiating a solution with your kids that allows trust and respect to continue to build. Do you demand all of their passwords and usernames, or do you help them understand you want to be part of their world? Rather than giving your younger son or daughter their own smartphone, consider giving him or her a phone without access to the Internet. Come to an understanding with your kids, and then remember to always knock on your child's "door" before entering.

Chapter 21

How Do I Respond to My Kids' "First Love"?

Do you remember your "first love"—"puppy love," they used to call it? Do you remember the first time you held hands or that first kiss? And do you remember how life seemed to almost come to an end when the one you "loved" no longer "loved" you? Looking back now it may seem silly, but at the time it was serious stuff.

Somehow many parents seem to forget how important those feelings were to them when they were young. Of course it wasn't true love, but we didn't know that back then, did we? And if someone had tried to tell us it wasn't true love, we would have felt belittled and disrespected. That is still true today with our kids.

As children grow they want us to regard them as mature (regardless of their age) and able to make their own decisions. It is simply not advantageous to tell our kids that the passion or heartache they feel now is only "puppy love." Sure, they will no doubt outgrow it and even look back on it with laughter later, but they don't want to hear that now. Our attitudes toward their "first love" will either convince them that we care and understand or that we don't have a clue about their world.

When we find our kids in this "lovesick" state of mind, instead of teasing them or minimizing their feelings, this is an ideal opportunity to engage in positive conversation. This is the time to take our child's first love experience seriously and *not* communicate that it's insignificant or premature. In reality, according to one study, it may even be the "most significant and intense love a person ever feels!"[1]

Take the time to explain that you too experienced these emotions, and that they are a significant indication that your child is growing up. Use this as a chance to talk about what real love is (see chapter 3). Communicate enthusiastic attitudes like "Tell me about it!" or "Isn't it exciting that you're beginning to feel these kinds of emotions *now*?" By supporting your kids through this stage, you are making a clear statement that you care about what is significant to them and that you are there for them. By indicating their feelings now, they will more likely seek your support again and again later.

Brain scientists at University College London scanned the brains of young lovers while they were thinking about their boyfriends and girlfriends and discovered that "four separate areas of the brain became very active. This affirms the notion that falling in love is an all-encompassing emotion that engages nearly every part of the mind and body."[2]

The National Campaign to Prevent Teen and Unplanned Pregnancy gathered responses from teens and published it in a selection called "Talking Back." One teenager pleaded: "Talk to us honestly about sex, love, and relationships. Just because we're young doesn't mean that we can't fall in love…These feelings are very real and powerful to us. Help us to handle the feelings in a safe way—without getting hurt or hurting others."[3]

By validating the real feelings your child has, he or she will feel supported, understood, and loved.

Chapter 22

What Sexual Rules or Boundaries Do I Set for My Child?

Rules are important. Boundaries are necessary. And we need to set them for our kids. But it is important to remember that "rules without relationship lead to rebellion." Place all the rules and boundaries within the context of your loving relationship with your kids. You might want to reread chapters 3, 4, and 5 of this book as you begin to set your child's boundaries.

As we said, whenever God tells us "no" or sets up boundaries for us, he does so out of two loving motivations—to provide for us and to protect us. As you set sexual rules and boundaries for your kids, let them know you have the same loving motivation as well.

I (Josh) have found the "umbrella illustration" a good way to explain the provide-and-protect nature of the rules.

I explain that the rules are like an umbrella. If it is raining outside you put up an umbrella. As long as you stay under that umbrella, you are under its protection and you are under its provision. You are protected from the rain and you are provided with dryness. But when by an act of your will you move out from underneath that umbrella, you have removed yourself from its protection and provision and you suffer the consequences. You get wet. There are consequences to your choices.

It is important that our kids sense that any boundaries we set up are because we love them and want them to be provided for and protected. With that as a foundation, then what are some excellent boundaries that need to be established? We offer five.

1. Dating Boundary

One big question we parents must face is when to let our kids start dating. Many adolescents begin quite young, as early as age 11 or 12. But just because "everybody else is dating" (which they are not at 11 or 12) is no reason to let your kids start dating then.

The time to allow your young person to date is when you as a parent are confident that your child is mature enough to date responsibly. This means your young person is ready to set some moral standards along the lines we mentioned in chapter 3, namely a commitment to purity, faithfulness, and the choice to express Godlike love. A young person needs to be able to clearly articulate these standards and stick to them. If your teen is not ready for committing to standards, he or she is not ready to say no to the pressures toward premarital sex. And such a child should certainly not be out dating.

Another issue to consider is the age difference between your young person and the one he or she wants to date. The Campaign to Prevent Teen and Unplanned Pregnancy rightly and emphatically urges that parents "take a strong stand against your daughter dating a boy significantly older than she is. And don't allow your son to develop an intense relationship with a girl much younger than he is."[1] They go on to say,

> Older guys can seem glamorous to a young girl. But the risk
> of matters getting out of hand increases when the guy is

much older than the girl. Try setting a limit of no more than a two (or at most three) year age difference. The power differences between older boys or men and younger girls can lead girls into risky situations, including unwanted sex.[2]

Glenn Stanton, director of Family Formation Studies at Focus on the Family, explains that "parents who set moderate, reasonable rules for teens experienced the lowest prevalence of sexual activity with their teens. These parents set moderate rules, carefully supervised their teenagers in regard to whom they dated and where they went, and insisted on a reasonable curfew."[3]

2. Entertainment-Media Boundaries

Research shows that "...teens who watch sexual content on television are more likely to engage in sex; teens who watch a lot of television tend to have negative attitudes about being a virgin; and teens that see sexual content as being reality are more impacted by the sexual content." In light of that statement, consider that "average students, for example, watch 5,000 hours of television before they ever get to school."[4] However, children now select the Internet over TV as their choice of entertainment.[5]

Boundaries need to be set as to the amount of time, when, and where our young people watch and engage in entertainment media.

3. Boundaries with Alcohol and Drugs

We constantly taught our children that when people take alcohol or drugs, they lose their freedom to not only make right moral choices, but to act responsibly. For example, look at the effects of drugs and alcohol on sexual intercourse or oral sex. A number of years ago the "Youth Risk Behavior Surveillance Report" showed the following: [6]

- Among currently sexually active students, 25.6 percent (30.9 percent of males and 20.7 percent of females) reported using drugs or alcohol during last intercourse.

- Among currently sexually active students, 25.4 percent of twelfth graders, 24.7 percent of eleventh graders, 27.7 percent of tenth graders, and 24 percent of ninth graders reported using drugs or alcohol during last intercourse.

- Among currently sexually active students, 17.8 percent of black students, 24.1 percent of Hispanic students, and 27.8 percent of white students reported using alcohol or drugs during last intercourse.

4. Home Alone Boundary

Studies show that teens usually have sex at home after school and before parents come home from work. Set a boundary that no friends of the opposite sex are to be in the house when no "adult" is present. They might scream, "You've got to be kidding! Mom and Dad, don't you trust me?" This is precisely when you want your child to know you really love them and want to provide for and protect them.

Education.com reports the following:[7]

- 75.1 percent of males and 59.4 percent of females left unsupervised for five or fewer hours per week reported having had sexual intercourse compared to 87.6 percent of males and 72.5 percent of females left unsupervised for 30 or more hours per week.

- 5.7 percent of males and 15.3 percent of females left unsupervised for five or fewer hours per week reported having had an STD compared to 13.6 percent of males and 19.5 percent of females left unsupervised for 30 or more hours per week.

• 43 percent of males and 27.9 percent of females reported last having had sexual intercourse in their own homes.

Some very practical words again from Harvest USA:

> *Overnight sleep-overs can be the Trojan horse for porn exposure or other sexual experimentation. Assume other families (even church families) do not take the techno dangers as seriously as you do. Make sure your teens have a clear plan of action (including calling home for a ride) if they find themselves in any compromising situations.*

5. Boundaries for the Computer, Cell Phone, Handheld Devices, and the Internet

More than 50 percent of web access is no longer through the "computer" but through handheld devices (smartphones, iPads, Kindles, and so on). Many parents require that the computer be in an open area of the house (and not the bedroom) and also require all Internet-accessing devices be placed in the parents' room at bedtime.

Harvest USA is a Christian ministry that aids churches and families in the area of helping kids say no to sexual pressure. They make the point that parents should

> *let your teens know you lovingly check-up on them and the techno-dangers to their walk with God. Give them "permission" to use your check-ups as a peer-pressure defeater. Then they can say, "I can't do that because I know my parents will find out." This can provide hedges of protection Christian teens actually crave.*[8]

In the Old West certain establishments enforced a "check your gun at the door" policy. The idea was to keep the place safer. One young mother had a helpful idea to protect her family in a similar way when her kids' friends visited. She instituted a "check your smartphone at the door" policy. She was aware that kids could save porn images on their phones and view them without the need of the Internet by use of an SD card. So to prevent porn viewing in her home she simply collected every smartphone up front then returned it as kids left the premises...just like establishments in the Old West did with guns.

In regard to Internet use on computers, Harvest USA urges,

> *Buy a quality Internet filter! It is unwise to have Internet access without some form of blocking and filtering device. Consider putting every family member using the Internet— Dad, Mom, each child—on an "accountability program" like Covenant Eyes that sends e-mail reports of inappropriate uses to accountability partners. You need to model accountability regarding your own use and may also want to set yourself up as one of your teen's accountability report recipients.*[9]

Note also that filtering programs are available for mobile devices as well.

We listed a number of "accountability" software programs in chapter 19, but we will repeat it here:

X3 Watch—pay/free	www.x3watch.com/
Total Net Guard—pay	http://afo.net/
Bsecure—pay	www.bsecure.com/
Net Nanny—pay	www.netnanny.com/
Covenant Eyes—pay	http://covenanteyes.com/

K9 Web Protection—free	www1.k9webprotection.com/
Safe Eyes—free	www.internetsafety.com/
Cyber Sitter—pay	www.cybersitter.com/
Pure Sight—pay	www.puresight.com/

Also:

> *Regularly check internet history, cell-phone and instant-messaging records, hits on YouTube; also examine MySpace [and Facebook] pages and who's on the friends list, and know the friends with whom your teen is playing MMORPG's (Massively Multiplayer Online Role Playing Games). Beware of allowing use of MySpace-type sites, where teens often experiment in building a double life, condition themselves to Internet false intimacy, or find their sense of belonging in a virtual community to the exclusion of the real world.*[10]

There are many other "boundaries" you need to establish in your family. One very critical boundary is related to sexual abuse, whether physical or verbal. In an article posted by *Health and Fitness* entitled "Teaching Children About Healthy Sexuality" it correctly explains that

> *parents have an important task of teaching kids to respect the individualized space and the sexual body parts of others. A no touching rule can be taught. "Please do not touch others on their sexual body parts." "Keep your hands to yourself." "If someone touches your sexual body parts, please tell me."*[11]

These are the kinds of boundaries we need to establish with and for our kids. Give your children permission to emphatically say "*no*" to anyone (even family members) who wants to touch "private parts." Constantly reinforce with them that it is not only okay to say "*no*," but it is important that they come to you if any touching like that occurs.

The boundaries you set up with and for your children are like the umbrella we spoke about. Every one of them is positive and becomes an act of your love to protect your child and to provide for him or her. Above all else let your kids know you are doing what you are doing because you love them. They may not like the boundaries or even fully understand your reasoning, but they can know you are doing it because you love them.

Chapter 23

How Realistic Is It to Expect Them to Wait?

Along a freeway in Los Angeles, California, stood a large billboard that read, "If you have to have sex, wear a condom." When I (Josh) saw that I thought to myself, *What do they mean, "Have to have sex"*? Is sex a necessary part of sustaining life? Does a person have to have sex, like we have to have water, to live?

Some years ago, a woman who went by the name of Dr. Ruth was wildly popular in the United States and around the world as a "sex expert." She was a small, elderly woman who was blunt, often humorous, and very popular as a university guest speaker.

During a question-and-answer period at the University of Cincinnati, a student asked her, "Dr. Ruth, what if you can't wait?" She replied, "Young man, it's unrealistic to expect you to wait. Your libido is too strong." The crowd broke out in a roar of applause.

In light of that answer, consider these questions: "What if my girlfriend doesn't want to do it, but I do?" Is it still unrealistic to expect a young man to wait? Doesn't Dr. Ruth say that the "libido is too strong"? So if a man has the "sex urge" we really can't expect him to wait, right? Then does that mean it is also unrealistic to expect a rapist to wait?

Dr. Ruth and an entire generation of young people need to realize we are human beings created in God's image, not animals driven by uncontrollable urges and instincts. Sexual involvement is a choice. I'm sure Dr. Ruth and a host of other "sex experts" would agree that *it is* realistic for a man to wait and restrain himself when a girl doesn't want to have sex with him. In fact, he is obligated by law not to force himself on a woman.

So is a man's libido too strong or isn't it? Our kids are told that if a young woman wants to have sex…then a young man's libido is too strong. But what if she doesn't want to have sex? Then is the young man's libido *not* too strong? Confusing? This type of sexual philosophy is inconsistent and simply isn't logical. With this approach, how can we expect these same young people (who are told they can't wait to have sex before marriage) to be faithful within marriage? If a married man finds another woman who wants to have sex with him, isn't it also unrealistic for him to be faithful to his wife because his libido is "too strong"?

We need to teach our young people that purity is realistic and is required by God and a moral society. We are to think with our mind, not with our pelvis. Sex is a matter of choice that results in consequences either positive or negative.

Lakita Garth, former Miss Black California, talked about sexual consequences in an interview:

> *I was in a commercial shoot a few years ago. It was a Fanta soft drink commercial and we were taking a break. This girl whom I didn't know turned to me and asked, "So Lakita, how's your sex life?" I was stunned that she would be so forward to ask such a question. I replied, "Excuse me, but I don't have a sex life."*
>
> *She then replied, "So tell me about your last sexual experience," and I said, "Well, I don't have a last sexual experience."*

*Her jaw seemed to hit the ground. She said, "I can't believe
with all the guys you've been with you haven't done it. Don't
you feel you've missed out on it all?"*

*I said, "You know what? You're right. I have missed out. I've
missed out on the thrill of waking up the next morning won-
dering if my pregnancy test strip was going to turn blue. I
missed out on walking into a clinic with my best friend holding my hand because chances are, my boyfriend's not going to
be there for me when I'm pregnant because all he wants is for
me to get an abortion. And I missed out on feeling like one of
my roommates, who every year around the same time, 'cele-
brates' a child that was never born in regretful tears because
she got an abortion.*

*"And I miss out on waking up in a bed, staring at the ceiling of
an AIDS hospice, like a good friend, Rod. Rod thought he was
the man! He was out there. He bought into the lie that everybody's doing it. When Rod was on his deathbed he begged me
to never stop doing what I'm doing now. So I guess you're right!
I have missed out on a lot!"*[1]

Choices have consequences. And when your kids choose not to
have sex before marriage and then remain faithful in marriage, they
thankfully miss out on a lot of pain and heartache. So it is not unrealistic to expect our young people to make right moral choices. We
earnestly need to teach them that living sexually pure and faithful
is how God instructs us to live and he does so to provide for us and
to protect us.

Chapter 24

How Do I Get My Kids to Treat the Opposite Sex Properly?

Does it concern you that so many young people lack sexual boundaries? Have you been in a mall and watched how some 12-, 13-, or 14-year-old kids act today? It's as if no one has taught them moral boundaries or how a boy should treat a girl. So how do you get your young daughter or son to grow up to treat the opposite sex appropriately? Because if you can teach them young how to respect the opposite sex, it will go a long way in helping them live in a morally pure way.

The most effective way to communicate this is by modeling love and respect within our own marriages. Kids are observing our attitudes and actions and learning how to respect or disrespect by how we treat one another.

And this may sound strange, but one of the best ways to teach your young daughter how to respect and treat the opposite sex is for her dad to take her on dates. This will also help her know what standards to expect in dating, in general. This had such a positive impact on our own daughters. Kelly, our oldest, writes this:

*When I was young, my dad would take my sisters and me
on dates and tell us, "If a boy doesn't treat you this way, then
you need to walk away from him." He would open the door
for us, be very polite, talk kindly and he would just model the
way that a man should respect a young woman. I can now
more fully understand what that really meant to me. Dating
was a time for me to get to know someone, not a time to feel
pressured into anything. Dates with my dad were his behind-
the-scenes way of making sure that I didn't feel pressured to
do anything that I wasn't comfortable doing. That one little
thing helped me avoid the pressure to cross my boundaries.*

Family and marriage counselor Dr. Corey Allan says: "If you're a father, take your daughter out on dates beginning now. Model how a man acts: hold the door for her, talk and listen to her, dress up for the date. This will set the bar high for her future dates. The same holds true for sons. Moms can take them out and model how a lady acts."[1]

Dad, take the time to schedule a daddy-daughter or daddy-son date occasionally. Go out to eat for a favorite meal or to do an activity your child enjoys. Mom, take your son out and do something together. Model before him how a woman wants to be treated. The best way you can teach your kids how to treat the opposite sex is by example. You become their model of how they should act.

Chapter 25

What About "Sexting," and What Can I Do About It?

Sexting is a form of texting where cell-phone users exchange pictures or videos of a graphic, sexual nature.

Here are some of the reality today's families are facing:

- 75 percent of 12-to-17-year-olds own cell phones, and 88 percent of those use text messaging. Teens send an average of 3146 texts per month, and kids ages 9 to 12 send 1146 texts a month.[1] While these statistics are shocking, they are not surprising. Cell phones are glued to the hands of kids everywhere, at school, at home, at the mall, and so on. And they are the technological tool used in "sexting." Did you know that:

- 20 percent of teens have sent or posted nude or seminude pictures or videos of themselves.
- 39 percent of teens have sent or posted sexually suggestive messages.

Of those who have sent or posted sexually suggestive messages:

- 71 percent of teen girls and 67 percent of teen boys say they sent or posted this content to a boyfriend or girlfriend.

- 21 percent of teen girls and 39 percent of teen boys say they have sent such content to someone they wanted to date.

- 66 percent of teen girls and 60 percent of teen boys say they did so to be "fun or flirtatious."

- 40 percent of teen girls say they sent sexually suggestive messages or images as "a joke."[2]

While teens may think sexting is just "flirty fun," it is actually considered a felony. Over the last few years, numerous teens have been prosecuted as sex offenders for sending and receiving sexual images on their phones. Legally, sexting is creating child pornography, and forwarding images is seen as trafficking in child pornography. Teens tend to think that sexting is a private thing, that no one else will see, but images are easily and commonly shared among their friends.

So What Can We Do?

Youth specialist Al Menconi provides us with five practical ideas and suggestions:

- Carefully evaluate whether or not your kids need texting on their cell phones.

- Make rules about when and where. No texting during meals, during class, on family outings. Oh, and turn the phone *off* at night!

- No texting while they should be concentrating on something else. This includes driving—nearly half of teens admit to texting while driving, walking, or having a conversation with someone else. In several states, texting while driving is against the law.

- Establish consequences for misuse—for example, cheating, inappropriate messages, sexual communication, and so on. These are all no-go's. Want to make your point? Take your kid's phone away for a week.

- If you suspect your kids aren't texting appropriately, you can always look at their messages. Yes, it feels like snooping, but our first job as parents is to ensure that our kids use powerful technologies safely and responsibly.[3]

God has created human beings as sexual beings. Our kids are going to express their sexuality, either in a healthy way or an unhealthy way. Sex educator Logan Levkoff says, "Kids are looking for ways to express their sexuality, especially when they're told, 'Don't go out and do it.' It's not a real surprise that teens use technology to express their sexuality...without doing anything physically."[4]

Rather than just giving our kids do's and don'ts, we can use the topic of sexting to engage them in a conversation about this phenomenon. Take these opportunities to teach your kids about God's design for sexuality. The two reasons our kids are most likely engaging in sexting in the first place is to express their sexuality and to fit in with their peers. In this vulnerable stage of life, they are longing to be accepted, just as we all long to be accepted. As you teach your kids about sex you are actually guiding them through their newly emerging sexual feelings. And, as you do, they will learn to express those feelings in healthy ways rather than expressing them inappropriately as it is so often done at school, on TV, or on the Internet.

Chapter 26

How Do I Help My Kids Resist Sexual Pressure?

Today's kids are under tremendous pressure to give in to sex before marriage. They need to understand that God created sex within the context of his image and that sex is to be lived within the context of boundaries; and they need to be taught these things within the context of relationships. This was thoroughly covered in the first five chapters of this book. But it is also important to equip our kids to anticipate the pressure lines or "come-ons" they are apt to get.

Social pressure or peer pressure is a very strong influence in the life of a teenager. The sexual come-ons our kids get are tough to resist or know how to handle if they don't see them coming. First help your young people understand these concepts:

- Not everyone is "doing it," even though it may seem like it.

- Refusing to have sexual intercourse does not make them a prude or a baby. It shows that they have carefully considered the pros and cons and have decided that sex before marriage is not morally right or in their best interest.

- Sexual intercourse does not transform adolescents into adults.

- Sexual intercourse is never a proof or test of love.

- Sexual relations will not solve the problems of a relationship that is in trouble.

- Increased self-esteem will help them resist peer pressure. Teens with a strong sense of self will not be as influenced by peer pressure as those desperately seeking approval and acceptance.

- There are "comebacks" that can be used when a young person is being pressured into behaving in ways that are not in their best interest.

The following comebacks to pressure lines can be most helpful to your teenager if you walk him or her through them bit by bit. Take one or two of them at a time and discuss them together. They can really make a difference.

Come-Ons and Comebacks[1]

Line	Comeback
"Aw c'mon, everybody does it!"	"I don't care, I'm not everybody. And besides, not everybody 'does it,' including some of the kids who say they do."
"If you loved me, you'd go to bed with me."	"If you loved me, you wouldn't pressure me into doing something that I don't want to do."
"If you loved me, you would…"	"Not a good reason for sex, but a good reason to walk away."[2]

"If you loved me you'd let me…"	"If you really loved me, you wouldn't ask!"
"If you don't, it means you don't love me."	"Just by saying that shows you don't love me."
"If you don't have sex with me, I'll break up with you."	"If being your girlfriend means that I have to sleep with you, then I guess I don't want to be your girlfriend."
"Don't you like me?"	"Yes, but I respect you too. You're beautiful/handsome, and I want to get to know you better."
"Sex will make us closer."	"Not if I'm worried about getting pregnant."
"Why won't you have sex with me?"	"Because I don't want to." (No further explanation needed.)
"Everyone is doing it."	"Then it shouldn't be too hard to find someone else."
"We had sex before—why are you turning me down now?"	"I'm entitled to change my mind. It's my body and my life, and I want to wait."
"Yo, let's do it. You know you want to!"	"No. No. No! What part of 'no' don't you understand? The N…or the O?"
"Your parents are out all night; let's go back to your house."	(Use your ace in the hole. Blame your folks.) "Go back to my house? We can't. My parents won't let me have boys over when they're not home."
"Get laid and be a man."	"I *am* a man!"
"Let me make a *man* out of you."	"What does sex have to do with being a man?"
"All your friends are doing it."	"Then go out with one of my friends."
"No one wants to marry an inexperienced girl."	"I guess I will be an exception."

"You don't know what you're missing."	"I guess that will make two of us."
"I can't help myself."	"If you can't help yourself now, how can you later?"
"I love you so much."	"Do you love me enough to wait?"
"It just happens."	"Sex doesn't just happen...it is a choice and don't you ever forget it."
"It's so beautiful."	"It's so beautiful that it's worth waiting for until marriage."
"But we're committed...doesn't that count?"	"Commitment is not marriage, but marriage is true commitment."

Chapter 27

How Does a Sexually Active Young Person Find a Clean Heart for a New Start?

Often when a young person does get involved sexually he or she feels guilt and shame or feelings of worthlessness. You have an opportunity and the great privilege to lead him or her to experience forgiveness—especially from God.

While sexual offenses generally occur between two people, the primary offense is against God. King David cried out in anguish to God, "Against you, and you alone, have I sinned; I have done what is evil in your sight" (Psalm 51:4). Why would David say this, and what was his sin?

God is gracious to give us examples of godly people messing up in *huge* ways throughout the Bible. David was the "man after God's own heart," yet he committed adultery with a woman named Bathsheba, got her pregnant, then had her husband killed on the front lines of battle. While David sinned against Bathsheba and her husband, he ultimately sinned against God. Why?

God created us for himself, to live in perfect friendship with him, to obey his good commandments, and to enjoy him through trusting and obeying him. And so when we do sin he convicts our hearts.

It is gracious for God to let us feel guilt and shame when we sin because it leads us to seeking forgiveness, which God gladly gives. Scripture says, "If we confess our sins, He is faithful and righteous to forgive us our sins and to cleanse us from all unrighteousness" (1 John 1:9 NASB).

It is true that all of us deserve punishment for our sins, but Scripture states that "[God] does not punish us for all our sins; he does not deal harshly with us, as we deserve. For his unfailing love toward those who fear him is as great as the height of the heavens above the earth. He has removed our sins as far from us as the east is from the west" (Psalm 103:10-12). Why did David say "as far from us as the east is from the west" rather than "as far as the north is from the south"?From east to west is a Hebrew expression for infinity. While you can measure the north from the south (there is a North Pole and a South Pole), you cannot measure the distance from the east to the west. If you go east or if you travel west, you will go on for eternity. This is the beautiful picture we need to give our young person of God's forgiveness. Let him or her know that God is always ready and willing to forgive.

Once an atmosphere of grace is established you can walk your young person through the following seven steps in order to experience the forgiveness that is available to him or her.

1. Call it sin. The first step toward forgiveness is to call their behavior what it is—sin. Help your young person realize that it was sin—something done outside of God's will. Recognizing something is sin is a prerequisite for confession.

2. Confess sin. The Bible says, "If we *confess* our sins, he is faithful and just to forgive us our sins and to cleanse us from all unrighteousness" (1 John 1:9 ESV). What does it mean to confess our sins? It means agreeing with God on two things: First, we are saying to

God, "Yes, it is sin." Second, we are acknowledging that God is just to forgive us our sins.

3. Acknowledge God's forgiveness. Have you ever heard others acknowledge their sin, faithfully confess it, but then walk away dejected, doubting that God could really forgive them for what they had done? Acknowledging and accepting God's forgiveness is a crucial step for our children to take. How can they forgive themselves if they don't believe God forgives them?

For many sexually active young people, this is the tough step. Despite God's promise in 1 John 1:9 to forgive us of all our sin, often young people who have had sex outside of marriage find it hard to believe the promise. They often feel cheap, used, and unworthy of God's love.

Help your young person realize that none of us deserve to be forgiven based on any of our actions or feelings. The basis for our forgiveness is not the level of our sin or our feelings about it. The basis for forgiveness is Christ's sacrifice. God knew we would sin. So he provided his Son, Jesus Christ, to take on human flesh and to go to the cross. On that cross, he declared, "It is finished"—and after his resurrection everything that was necessary for us to be forgiven had been done. When our children accept Christ's forgiveness for their sexual sin, they agree that God's grace—evident in Christ's death and resurrection—is sufficient payment for their sin.

4. Forgive yourself. Often people will confess sin and acknowledge that God has forgiven them, but they do not forgive themselves. Our children may do the same thing. After sexual sin, they can start walking through life with a guilt that is not from God. It is self-produced.

Within the loving environment of forgiveness that we've established, we must remind our children of Christ's forgiveness of them.

Help them recognize the guilt they may be experiencing is a false guilt or self-condemnation. And we overcome self-condemnation with a heart of gratitude. Lead your child in praises and thanks to God for his loving forgiveness. A grateful heart can receive God's grace to the point of removing our sense of self-condemnation.

5. Bring forth fruit of repentance. You seldom hear someone talk about this fifth step. Yet it is one of the most critical in experiencing God's forgiveness and renewed relationships, especially in the sexual arena. The Bible says, "Prove by the way you live that you have repented" (Matthew 3:8). We must encourage our children not only to take the step of fully embracing forgiveness for their sexual sin, but to make daily choices to keep from returning to it. Repentance is an act of the will, not only to turn from sin, but to take active steps toward positive relationships with God and others.

6. Find someone to hold you accountable. Every one of us ought to have another person who loves us in Christ, who we trust, who can see if there is sexual immorality or impurity in our lives and can hold us accountable. We need one another—if a girl, then a girl—if a boy, then another young man—individuals who have relationships with Christ who can hold one another accountable.

Encourage your young person to have someone who can hold him or her accountable. If that isn't you, then encourage your child to select a person who is strong in his or her faith to be that accountability partner.

7. Go to the other person and ask for forgiveness. Whenever we become involved physically with someone outside of the boundary of marriage, we sin against that person too. Encourage your young person to go to that other person, and ask him or her for forgiveness for what happened. This can bring healing to that relationship that puts it on a higher, purer level, where it needs to be.

God convicts us and our children of our sin because he loves us. As parents, when our children sin, we have an opportunity to minister to them by walking them through the steps of forgiveness.

Chapter 28

Most Kids Don't Believe Oral Sex Is Having Sex. How Do I Correct Their Misconception?

There is a lot of confusion about the topic of oral sex. Is oral sex really considered sex? Why do kids engage in it? Are you still a virgin if you engage in oral sex? Can you get an STD from oral sex? What does the Bible say about it? What can parents do about it? Let's answer these questions.

What Is Oral Sex?

The dictionary defines *sex* as "sexually motivated phenomena or behavior." Whatever involves a sex organ is sex. Does oral sex result in the arousal, stimulation, and gratification of sexual organs? The answer is yes. Your body reacts to oral sex the same way it reacts to intercourse. Your hormones are aroused, your sexual organs respond, your brain is washed in neurochemicals that work like super glue to bond you to your partner, and you receive a blast of dopamine that makes you crave more of the same behavior. Your body thinks it's sex, your brain thinks it's sex, and your heart thinks it's sex. The following four types of physical contact are considered sex, because they cause both a physical and chemical reaction in your body:

1. oral-genital (oral sex)

2. manual-genital (sexual touching)

3. genital-genital

4. penetration

All four of these situations create a bond between partners and put a person at risk of infection from sexually transmitted disease. If a person engages in any of these four activities, he or she is considered sexually active.

What do kids believe about oral sex?

- 4 in 5 college students don't believe oral sex is sex.[1]

- 80 percent of today's young adults don't believe that oral sex should be considered as "having had sex."[2]

- Half of all teens ages 15 to 17 do not believe that oral sex is "sex."[3]

- Kids think of oral sex as a safe way to enjoy some of the benefits of vaginal sex with less risk of feeling guilty, getting a bad reputation, or going against their own values and beliefs.[4]

- 40 percent of adolescents consider oral sex to be "safer" sex, while 20 percent of teens do not know that STD transmission can occur through oral sex.[5]

How many kids engage in oral sex?

- Some 36 percent of teens ages 15 to 17 admit to having had oral sex. These numbers increase among teens and young adults ages 15 to 24.[6]

• About 75 percent of teens ages 15 to 17 who have had intercourse have also had oral sex, while 13 percent of teens ages 15 to 17 who have never had intercourse acknowledge engaging in oral sex.[7]

• Nearly 25 percent of tenth-graders in a school district in New England reported having multiple oral-sex partners within the last year. The females reported having three to four partners.[8]

Why do kids engage in oral sex?

• Students are tempted to have oral sex because of social pressure. More than 92 percent of teens think being a virgin in high school is good.[9] But, in the eyes of many teens, they can have oral sex and still remain virgins. One-quarter of sexually active adolescents report engaging in oral sex as a strategy to avoid intercourse.[10]

• Oral sex is becoming so common among teens that many only consider it "third base." Peer pressure undeniably plays a large role. Guys are often the initiators of oral-sex encounters, but more and more girls are willingly participating. Girls with lower self-esteem will often engage in oral sex just to remain in the group or to keep guys from leaving them.

Can STDs spread through oral sex?

• Oral sex has been associated with gonorrhea, syphilis, herpes, and HPV.[11]

• If, over their entire lifetime, a person has oral sex with five or more people, his or her chances of getting throat cancer are increased 250 percent.[12] That risk is increased 450 percent for people who have had oral sex with more than six partners.[13]

- Having had an oral HPV infection makes a person *3200 percent* more likely to get throat cancer.[14]

As a Parent, What Can You Do?

First, clearly define what sex is with your young people. Educate them about the health risks associated with oral sex, and make them aware of the long-term effects on their reputation and self-esteem. It is so important to understand youth culture, and to know the world your children are living in each day. The temptations and pressure are high for them to engage in oral sex. There are lasting consequences of engaging in oral sex, and choosing to engage in oral sex as an alternative to intercourse won't keep the memories of those sexual encounters from being paper-clipped to one's brain.

God's design for us is not to be sexually active while "preserving our virginity." Again, explain the reasons why God created sex and its place and purpose to your children as covered in the first section of this book. In Ephesians, Paul says, "Among you there must not be even a hint of sexual immorality, or of any kind of impurity… because these are improper for God's holy people" (Ephesians 5:3 NIV). God doesn't give us permission to engage in *some* sexual activities outside of marriage while avoiding others. He calls us to flee from all sexual immorality, and his motivation is to protect us and to provide the opportunity for maximum sex and intimacy within marriage.

Chapter 29

How Does a Healthy Self-Image Protect My Child from Premarital Sex?

Following are insights from two teenage boys:

I used premarital sex to deal with my lack of self-esteem. Each time it proved to me that I was a man and equipped me with good stories for the locker room.

I looked to female attention for proof of my worth as a male. The attention I received from a young lady became the gauge for my own worth.

Although both of these statements are from young men, young women with low self-esteem tell similar stories. They become involved sexually to "prove" their worth, to "prove" they can please another person, to "prove" they are attractive to the opposite sex, and to bolster their self-esteem by having experiences to describe to their peers.

Other young people, however, become sexually active as a way of reinforcing their low view of themselves. We tend to act in harmony with how we see ourselves. Our self-image is like a set of lenses through which we view all of life. Based on what we see through those lenses, we make choices about what to think and how to act.

If an adolescent girl, for example, has low self-esteem and is feeling pressured to become sexually involved, it is easy for her to think, when she looks through her distorted lenses, *I'm not worth much anyway, so what difference does it make? This is what bad people do.* Soon such a young person is acting out her low opinion of herself.

We are living in a culture that teaches a child that she is only as good as she looks when compared to a beautiful woman on a magazine cover. Heightened self-consciousness regarding body image is not only foisted upon our girls, but our young boys as well. Focus on the Family youth specialist Rob Jackson reminds us that, as parents,

> *We have the power to affirm the immutable worth of our children because of what God the Father sacrificed on their behalf: the life of Jesus Christ. The child's performance and the approval of others will no longer be a measuring stick for the worth of their lives. The performance of Christ on behalf of our child, and the Father's approval of that child who embraces Christ, confirms the worth that must be learned not only intellectually, but also emotionally.*[1]

Our children are special, not because of anything spectacular they have done or are doing, but because of whom God created them to be and what he has done on their behalf. When parents model this value based on God, it has a tremendous positive impact on a child's self-esteem.

The National Campaign to Prevent Teen Pregnancy reports that "parents and family members have no choice about their influence in helping develop the self-esteem of their children and family members—their only choice is whether they do it well or poorly."[2] Studies show that when children feel valued by their families, "it reduces the risk for serious major depression at age 18."[3] Also, feeling valued at age 9 "positively predicts self-esteem and reduces the risk for depression (especially for males), drug abuse—dependence, thoughts of suicide, interpersonal problems, withdrawn and anxious-depressed behavior, and delinquent and aggressive behavior."[4]

Praise your children for the highly valued individuals they are. Let them know that God values them as well. Speak the following truths from God to them often. Say, "You are special and of great value because God says that

- you are loved (John 3:16),

- you are his child (John 1:12),

- you are chosen (Ephesians 1:4),

- you are forgiven (Ephesians 1:7),

- you are his masterpiece (Ephesians 2:10),

- you are his friend (John 15:15), and

- you are protected by him (1 John 5:18)."

In a culture where truth is seen as unknowable, where reason has overshadowed faith, and where naturalistic science has become the sole basis of reality, children more than ever need confidence in the one unchangeable reality that God is their Creator and the one who loves and accepts them without condition. Our children are tempted to put their worth in what their peers think of them, in their grades, their experience, and their talents and abilities. But you have the greatest influence in your children's lives. Let them know often that you think the world of them, and constantly remind them how God loves and cares for them.

The relationship you have with your kids is one of the most important keys to helping them say no to sexual involvement. If the relationship is good, if you really connect with them lovingly, your kids are far more likely to have a healthy self-image and realize the boundaries you set for them are to provide for and protect them. When you instruct your kids within the context of a loving relationship you are helping them develop a healthy self-image and giving them added strength to stand strong in the midst of a destructive culture.

Chapter 30

Six Ways to Become Wise Parents Who Talk to Their Kids About Sex

Raising your kids in today's world to resist sexual pressure is not easy. We have given you some tips and strategies in this book to do just that, and we hope you have found them valuable. And as we pointed out in the first section, the relationship you have with your children is key. *How* you interact with your kids is just as important, if not more so, as *what* you interact about. So to conclude our journey together we would like to provide six ways to become a wiser, more effective parent in helping your kids experience their sex lives as God designed them to experience it.

We as parents can tell you that these six have worked for us and we have seen how effective they have been for others.

1. Be an "Askable" Parent

As much as this might get our stomachs flipping, being available for any question your child asks is important. If your children are asking you the questions, then you are in a position to guide them. The key here is to be as calm as possible with any questions your kids might ask and be honest and candid with your answers.

For example, when our daughter Katie was 13 years old, I (Josh) was driving through the mountains with her and her friend Sarah. As I was watching them in the backseat in the rearview mirror, I saw them whispering back and forth, glancing at me, then whispering more. I knew something big was coming.

Sure enough, Katie jumped into the front seat, Sarah stuck her head between our seats, and Katie said, "Dad, I have a question. It's no big deal." That told me it *was* a big deal! "Dad, what's oral sex?" I almost swerved off the road! She was only in eighth grade! I was blindsided—but I couldn't show it. So I told her exactly what it was. When I finished, she exclaimed, "Gross!" and hopped back into the backseat with Sarah.

Now, I was worried about how this conversation could get relayed to Sarah's mom later that day. I told Dottie what had happened the second I got home. Then, I called Sarah's mom and explained to her how the conversation came up and everything that I said. There was a long pause on the other end of the phone, and I was thinking, *Oh no! I've said too much to someone else's child!* Then came a huge sigh, and she said, "Oh, thank God that they asked *you!*"

Be an "askable" parent. Let your children know they can talk to you about anything, anytime. Even if you feel uncomfortable with the questions, try to not let your kids sense it. If they sense discomfort in you, they will tend to think that the subject is taboo. But when they sense you are an "askable" parent you will have the wonderful opportunity to be there first to guide and direct them in their unfolding understanding of sex as God designed it.

2. Be a "Listening" Parent

When we listen attentively to our kids, it tells them they are important and we want to hear what they have to say. You really can't be a very good "askable" parent without being a good "listening" parent.

To reinforce to your child that you're a good listener, try to stop what you're doing and look directly at him or her. You can't always do that, but when you do it signals to them that you're listening and what he or she is about to say is important to you.

Many parents tell us that they want to be good listeners, but their kids just don't talk a lot to them. This is where you asking them questions can get them talking. Asking your kids questions can

- show them respect and confirm that you value their input

- let you know just how much they know or don't know about a subject

- help you see if they have accurate knowledge

- help to clarify statements or topics of conversation

- provide you time to formulate an answer

- help you evaluate your child's maturity.

The following are some typical questions that can guide you through conversations with your child.

1. Have you ever seen something online that made you uncomfortable or curious?

2. How did that happen? How did it make you feel?

3. Have any of your friends ever accessed pornography—accidentally or intentionally?

4. What do you think about…?

5. What have you heard about…?

6. Can you tell me what you already know about…?

Simple questions like these can open up a dialogue with your child and then you can demonstrate you are a good listener.

3. Be a Parent with Values

As we stated in chapter 4, relationships are the fertile ground in which your young people's beliefs grow that in turn shapes their values that drives their actions. Your kids make decisions about their sexual behavior based on their values. And, by and large, they get their first set of values from you. That is why it is so important that you be a parent with strong biblical values.

Values are simply personal truths that we base decisions, attitudes, and actions on. And as a parent you have the responsibility and best opportunity of anyone to impart your values to your children.

One case study showed that "26 percent of adolescents said the main reason why they do not have sex is because of religion, morals, and values."[1]

Writing in *The Most Effective Deterrent*, Glenn Stanton reinforces the power of passing on your values to your children:

> *Permissive parental values regarding adolescent sexual behavior emerged as a strong risk factor for both males and females. Not surprisingly, adolescents who perceived their parents as accepting of premarital adolescent sexual activity were more likely to be sexually experienced.*[2]

In a nationally representative survey, "64 percent of teens report morals and values are equally important as health information and services in influencing teen sexual behavior, while nearly one-quarter of teens (23 percent) say that morals and values are more influential."[3]

Take the time to make a list of the main values you hold about sexual relations. To help you develop your list, ask yourself the following questions and write down your answers.

1. What are the values I hold about sex that my child needs to know about it?

2. Why do I believe them to be true?

3. What difference have these values made in my life?

4. What difference can these values make in my child's life?

The following is just a list of possible value areas to consider. Perhaps this list will trigger ideas for you and your family:

• sex in marriage	• God is love
• children are a gift from the Lord	• love one another
• created in the image of God	• love people vs. loving things
• friendship	• respect
• loyalty	• integrity
• purity	• honesty
• faithfulness	• trustworthiness
• the Bible is God's truth for us	• relationships
• sex is beautiful	• pregnancy
• behavior	• marriage
• dating or courtship	• reverence
• how we dress	• a wedding

Once you have identified your key values, take the time to naturally and casually share them with your children.

4. Be a Parent Who Befriends Your Kids' Friends

At about 5:30 p.m. they all started to show up. I (Dottie) was about seven years old and had taken it upon myself to throw a dinner party. The only problem was that I'd failed to mention all this to my mom. But, instead of getting angry or sending the kids home, she enthusiastically set the table and opened up some boxes of macaroni, cans of peas, and some cans of fruit. It was all she had in the cupboard, but we had a feast and a great celebration! And as always, she made it a point to focus on each child that came. She purposely made each one feel welcome and special. Mom got involved in the lives of my friends, whether it was convenient for her or not, and it made a huge impact on their lives as well as on mine. In fact, my mom became my friends' hero.

Think back on your childhood. Which of your friends' parents did you enjoy the most? Why did you enjoy them? How did they influence you?

I specifically remember two parents of my friends that had an impact on me—one negative and one very positive.

Growing up, I had one particular friend that I hung out with from the first through the seventh grade. We were in the same Brownie and Girl Scout troops, took baton lessons together, swimming classes, sewing lessons, and so on. After seventh grade I moved out of state, but I came back to visit her when I was in the ninth grade.

I clearly remember running up to her front door after being gone for a year. I could hardly wait to see her again. Her mom, however, answered the door before my friend arrived, so I visited with her for a few moments. I don't remember much about the beginning of that conversation except that I asked her if she'd had a good year while I was away. She told me that she did, and went on to state that "for the very *first* time," she and her husband had enjoyed having their daughter's friends in their home. She made it a point to articulate that they had *"never"* liked her daughter's friends before, but went on to explain that they loved the kids that she had brought home this past year.

I remember feeling stunned. I felt embarrassed and hurt and wished I could somehow evaporate. For seven years I had been a guest in her home! So, *why* she told me this I will never know! But it was humiliating and painful. And, to this very day when I think of her, *that statement* is the most vivid memory I have of her. Often I have wondered what I did during so many years of being with her daughter that caused her to say such a cruel thing.

On the other hand, there was a mom of one of my friends up the street who was crazy about me. And it was obvious! When I would have a tap-dancing recital, she was the one who would come over to curl my hair. She came with my family and even took pictures. When I think of her, I remember how special she always made me feel and how much happiness she always expressed when I went over to her house. What a contrast!

How do you want to be remembered by your children's friends? Get involved with your kids' friends and choose to have a positive impact. As you do it can

1. make a statement to your child that people who are important to them are important to you

2. help you understand who is having an influence on your child

3. put you in a position where your kids and their friends will want to communicate with you and listen to your opinions, which will most likely reduce negative peer pressure that your child's friends will have on him or her

Our youngest daughter, Heather, was going to a ball game with a young man that I (Josh) was not that familiar with. I spoke to her about my reservations. Her immediate reply was, "Dad, relax. He so respects you he wouldn't do anything you didn't approve of."

Be a hero to your kids' friends. It often doesn't require much to achieve this status because most kids don't expect their friends' parents to notice them much. I (Josh) would always take time to talk to the kids our son or daughters brought over to the house. I would just introduce myself, sit down, and take some time with them to let them know I cared about who they were, what they liked, and how glad I was that they were visiting.

I also made a special point to meet the kids on any sports team in which my own kids were active. I'd let them know I'd be rooting for them and even took the time to give them some "pointers" about the game if I had some experience in that sport. This kind of hero status will have a direct impact on your own kids and on your relationships with your kids' friends as well.

5. Be a Parent Who Networks with Other Parents

Networking with other parents gives you the opportunity to gain from their knowledge. By interacting with other like-minded people who have similar interests, experiences, and goals you can pick up valuable tips on raising your own kids. Some of the greatest practical knowledge and insights come from other parents with children about the same ages or just a little older than yours, and even parents who have already raised their children. You can find encouragement, parenting ideas, companions for your own kids, educational tools, sports or entertainment suggestions, as well as advice on discipline, health issues, and sex education.

When I (Dottie) became a mom, one of my closest friends had

five children. I watched every move she made. She was an outstanding mother. Because two of her children were older than ours, I'd go to her to get ideas with each new stage. She was an ongoing encouragement to me. She gave me perspective on what was important and what really wasn't. I remain grateful to this day! Finding other parents you trust, admire, and respect is like discovering a treasure chest overflowing with invaluable jewels.

There are a number of national organizations that you also might want to network with. For mothers of preschoolers, I suggest MOPS International (Mothers Of Preschoolers) found at MOPS.com. It is their goal to help meet the needs of mothers and preschoolers from conception through kindergarten. Three of our daughters have found this to be very helpful.

My youngest daughter recommends Stroller Strides (at stroller strides.com), a fitness program for moms and babies. For parents looking for places to meet other moms and to introduce sports and physical exercise in a fun and safe environment, both The Little Gym (www.littlegym.org) and Mommy and Me (www.mommyandme. com) are groups our daughters have enjoyed with their kids.

Another excellent resource is a group called Moms in Prayer International (formerly "Moms In Touch"—see momsintouch.org). Their mission is to have a worldwide impact for Christ on children and schools by gathering mothers to pray.

We are convinced that there is strength in numbers, so networking with other parents who have similar values can spark ideas, and can be a helpful give-and-take in sharing effective teaching strategies (especially in the area of sex education). Let's face it. It takes courage to talk to kids about sex. We haven't met any parents who haven't trembled at the thought, and haven't wondered exactly what to say and how to say it. This is why networking is so essential.

6. Be a Parent Who Dreams with Your Kids

Parenting and children's health writer Laura Flynn McCarthy wrote an article in *Family Circle* and said, "Kids who feel they have a promising future are the most deliberate in preventing pregnancy... Hope is a great contraception."[4]

God told the children of Israel, "I know the plans I have for you... They are plans for good not for disaster, to give you a future and a hope" (Jeremiah 29:11). God was a champion of his people. It made them feel special and motivated them to live up to his expectations.

When we champion our kids and dream their dreams it raises them to a whole new level of hope and they end up wanting to live up to high expectations. King Solomon said, "Hope deferred makes the heart sick, but when dreams come true, there is life and joy" (Proverbs 13:12 NLT).

Growing up, my (Dottie) hero in life was Peter Pan. The story of Peter Pan is a wonderful tale about a little boy who never grows up. Of course, one of the great things about Peter was that he could fly. In the story—I'm sure you remember—is a charming character, a tiny fairy named Tinkerbell. One of the amazing abilities Tinkerbell had was to sprinkle magic pixie dust on people, which enabled them to fly like Peter Pan.

As a child, this story took my breath away. It captured my heart and my imagination, and I listened to it over and over. I dreamed about it, talked about it, sang about it, and lived it! Each time I thought about the boy who could fly I felt inspired and energized.

When I was about five years old, I clearly remember wandering downstairs into our basement. There, by the washing machine, I spotted a huge box of laundry detergent called Ivory Snow. Each granule of this soap was shaped like a snowflake. I suddenly got an incredible idea.

I could relive the scene in the story where Tinkerbell spreads magic pixie dust on Wendy, Michael, and John so that they could fly like Peter Pan. What a brilliant thought! So, with great delight and passion, I took handfuls and handfuls of Ivory Snow, which to me had become pixie dust, and spread it all over the entire basement. Now, decades later, I can still vividly remember the exhilaration of that experience. It was an unforgettable moment. When I was done, the entire basement was covered with soap!

Moments later I heard the basement door open…and then I heard footsteps on the stairs. It was my mom! I can just imagine what a lot of moms would have said. Things like:

- *What* is the matter with you?

- *What* were you thinking?

- You wasted *all that soap*?

- Do you have any idea *how much* all that soap costs?

- What a mess! I am *so angry* with you!

- Just *wait* until your father gets home!

- Clean this up—*this moment*!

- If you ever do anything like this again, you'll be grounded for *a year*!

But not my mom! She laughed hysterically, scooped me up, put me on her lap, and asked me what it all meant! When I told her it was Tinkerbell's pixie dust, she insisted that I tell her the whole story all over again. We both laughed and then later—*lightheartedly*—cleaned up the mess together.

What this experience reinforced to me was that my mom really loved me, that she loved being my mom, and that she loved taking care of me. But mostly it spoke so loudly that my mom *dreamed my dreams.* It said that what was important to me was important to her (in spite of any inconveniences to her!). That kind of dreaming together allowed me to have hope for the future—a secure hope.

Enter Their World

Dream with your children and enter into their worlds. The sky is the limit in creative ways to communicate your unshakable support. This step, when taken consistently throughout the growing-up process, can help to set the stage for open communication, which is especially important as your child approaches the pre-teen and teen years when sexual issues need to be frequently addressed.

Research confirms that "youth respond to the challenge of high expectations by making positive choices and setting goals for their future."[5] We need to help our young people pursue options for their futures that are more appealing than early pregnancy and parenthood.

Studies show that young people with high expectations and a sense of a bright future are "more than six times less likely to have sex."[6]

Be excited about your kid's hopes and dreams. But in doing so be sure it is their dreams you are helping them pursue—not yours. I (Dottie) learned that some dreams were my own, not my kids'.

When Sean was in the eighth grade, he had been playing baseball for several years. And, even if I do say so myself, he was good! When the spring rolled around, he mentioned to me that he had decided not to play that year. I well remember trying to talk him into playing. I argued that if he ever had any thoughts of playing high-school baseball, he had better play in eighth grade or he might lose ground and not be able to compete. He said he didn't care because he wanted to play basketball instead. I tried, very hard, to get him to care. He just didn't. I hate to admit this, but I first resorted to logic. That didn't work. So I then tried using emotion. That didn't work either! You ask, why was this so important to me? It's a simple answer—baseball was my love. I had been a passionate Red Sox fan growing up. (I *still* am!)

I love baseball! And I pictured Sean playing baseball because it was so important to me. When I finally came to grips with the reality that it was my love and not his, I backed off and encouraged him to pursue the sport he loved—basketball. Now, I'm sure grateful that he did because, to our whole family's enormous joy, he was able to play all through high school and all through college. And cheering for him at his games is something that makes some of our family's fondest memories.

Just as we know what is important to us, our kids know what is important to them. And it's our privilege and our "opportunity" to support them and to encourage them to follow their own dreams, not ours.

Find ways to promote a sense of future goals, dreams, ambitions, and career opportunities. A bright future encourages your kids to make "right choices."

Be an "askable" and "listening" parent, one with values, who befriends your kids' friends, networks with other parents, and dreams with your kids. As you learn and grow to become more and more of that kind of dad or mom, it will have a direct effect upon your kids' receptiveness to your teaching about sex.

Let us know about your progress in your journey of talking with your children about sex. Visit us at www.josh.org. There are also additional resources there that we hope will help you. We want to continue to be a service to you. And as you prayerfully raise your kids, may they live as "children of God without fault in a crooked and depraved generation, in which [they] shine like stars in the universe" (Philippians 2:15 NIV).

Josh and Dottie McDowell

For further research, documentation,
and critical insights on each chapter,
go to www.josh.org/straighttalk.

About the Authors and the Josh McDowell Ministry

As a young man, **Josh McDowell** was a skeptic of Christianity. However, while at Kellogg College in Michigan, he was challenged by a group of Christian students to intellectually examine the claims of Jesus Christ. Josh accepted the challenge and came face-to-face with the reality that Jesus was in fact the Son of God, who loved him enough to die for him. Josh committed his life to Christ, and for 50 years he has shared with the world both his testimony and the evidence that God is real and relevant to our everyday lives.

Josh received a bachelor's degree from Wheaton College and a master's degree in theology from Talbot Theological Seminary in California. He has been on staff with Campus Crusade for Christ for almost 50 years.

Dottie McDowell has been married to Josh for over 40 years. She has written several children's books with her husband, and she and Josh are enjoying their four adult children and eleven grandchildren as he continues to travel worldwide in his ministry. Dottie and Josh live in Southern California.

NOTES

Chapter 1—Just One Click Away

1. In reference to first five items in column: Nayeli E. Rodriguez and Number 17, NYC, "Exactly How Much Are The Times A-Changin'?," *Newsweek*, July 26, 2010, p.56; article sources: Blogpulse, Google Official History, Reality Blurred, The NPD Group, NBC, Bowker, USPS, The Radicati Group, FORBES, Nielsen, Newspaper Assoc. of America, Digital Music News, Apple, iTunes.

2. Matt McGee, "By The Numbers: Twitter Vs. Facebook Vs. Google Buzz," SearchEngine Land, February 23, 2010, http://search engineland.com/by-the-numbers-twitter-vs-facebook-vs-google-buzz-36709.

3. "Internet 2010 in numbers," Royal Pingdom, January 12, 2011, http://royal.pingdom.com/2011/01/12/internet-2010-in-numbers/.

4. "Internet 2010."

5. Horace Dediu, "iTune app total downloads (finally) overtook song downloads," ASYMCO, July 13, 2011, www.asymco.com/2011/07/13/itunes-app-total-downloads-finally-overtook-song-downloads/.

6. Madeeha Azam, "Internet 2010 in Numbers [Summary]," Pro Pakistani, January 27, 2011, http://propakistani.pk/2011/01/27/Inter net-2010-in-numbers-summary/.

7. "That Facebook friend might be 10 years old, and other troubling news," *Consumer Reports* magazine, June 2011, www.consumer reports.org/cro/magazine-archive/2011/june/electronics-computers/state-of-the-next/facebook-concerns/index.htm.

8. *The Foster Letter*, May 25, 2011, p. 4.

9. As reported at Wikipedia.org/wiki/Wikipedia.

10. As reported at Wikipedia.org/wiki/Wikipedia.

11. Mickey Alam Khan, "Internet Overtakes TV As Preferred Medium For Under-24 Crowd," *Direct Marketing News,* July 25, 2003, www.dmnews .com/internet-overtakes-tv-as-preferred-medium-for-under-24-crowd/ article/81588.

12. Michael D. Resnick, PhD, et al., "Protecting Adolescents from Harm: Findings from the National Longitudinal Study on Adolescent Health," *Journal of the American Medical Association,* September 10, 1997 (vol. 278, no. 10), p. 829.

13. Family Safe Media as reported at familysafemedia.com/pornogra phy_statistics.html#anchor5, 2011.

14. Family Safe Media.

15. Family Safe Media.

16. Michael Leahy, *Porn University: What College Students Are Really Saying About Sex on Campus* (Chicago: Northfield Publishing, 2009), pp. 154-155.

17. Chiara Sabina, Janis Wolak, and David Finkelhor, "The Nature and Dynamics of Internet Pornography Exposure for Youth," *CyberPsychology & Behavior,* 2008 (vol. 11, no. 6), pp. 1-2.

18. Ed Vitagliano, quoted in "Caught! Online Porn, Predators Threaten Children, Teens," *American Family Association Journal,* January 2007, www.afa journal.org/2007/january/0107/caught.asp.

19. Focus on the Family Poll, October 2003, quoted in Rebecca Grace, "When Dad Falls: A Family's Ordeal with Pornography," Agape Press. Web. 25 Nov. 2009, www.crosswalk.com/1284103/.

20. Archdiocese of Omaha's Anti-Pornography Task Force, as reported at www.archomaha.org/pastoral/se/pdf/PornStats.pdf, 2011.

21. Family Safe Media.

22. Patricia M. Greenfield, "Inadvertent Exposure to Pornography on the Internet: Implications of Peer-to-Peer File-Sharing Networks for Child Development and Families," *Journal of Applied Developmental Psychology,* Nov./Dec. 2004 (vol. 25, no. 6), pp. 741-750, Web. 4 Dec. 2009, www.center-school.org/pko/documents/Inadvertentexposure.pdf.

Chapter 4—Sex: Taught Within the Context of Relationships

1. Archdiocese of Omaha's Anti-Pornography Task Force, www .archomaha.org/pastoral/se/pdf/PornStats.pdf, 2011.

2. The Commission on Children at Risk, *Hardwired to Connect: The Scientific Case for Authoritative Communications,* (New York: Broadway Publications, 2003).

3. *Hardwired to Connect.*

4. Caroline Bedell Thomas, MD, Karen Rose Duszynski, BA, and John Whitcomb Shaffer, MSc, PhD, "Family Attitudes Reported in Youth as Potential Predictors of Cancer," *Psychosomatic Medicine,* vol. 41, no. 4 (June 1979), pp. 287-302.

5. Carl Zimmer, "Friends with Benefits," *Time* magazine, February 20, 2012, p. 39.

6. Caitlin Flanagan, "Why Marriage Matters," *Time* magazine, July 13, 2009, p. 47.

7. "Back to School 1999—National Survey of American Attitudes on Substance Abuse V: Teens and Their Parents," The Luntz Research Companies and QEV Analytics, August 1999 as quoted in Lori Lessner, "Dads key against drugs, study finds," *Dallas Morning News,* August 31, 1999, p. 9A.

8. People Weekly, "Higher Learning: At Oxford University, Michael Jackson bares his soul and a plan to help kids," *People* magazine, March 19, 2001, p. 65.

Chapter 5—The 7 A's: The Building Blocks of Relationships

1. "Ten Tips for Parents: To Help Their Children Avoid Teen Pregnancy," The National Campaign to Prevent Teen and Unplanned Pregnancy, Date accessed: Feb 6, 2012, http://www.thenationalcampaign.org/resources/toTips.aspx.

Chapter 6—Who or What Most Influences Your Child's Behavior?

1. "Teens Look to Parents More Than Friends for Sexual Role Models," *ScienceDaily,* June 15, 2011, www.sciencedaily.com/ releases/2011/06/110615120355.htm.

2. Jeffrey Rosenberg and W. Bradford Wilcox, "The Importance of Fathers in the Healthy Development of Children," U.S. Department of Health and Human Services, 2006, www.childwelfare.gov/pubs/usermanuals/fatherhood/fatherhood.pdf.

3. "Teens Look to Parents."

4. David White, "Take Courage! Parents and the dreaded conversation," Center for Parent/Youth Understanding, 2008, www.cpyu.org/Page.aspx?id=338336.

5. "Trends in Teen Sexual Behavior," Current Thoughts and Trends online, May 2004.

6. B.M. King and J. Lorusso, "Discussions in the Home about Sex: Different Recollections by Parents and Children," *Journal of Sex & Marital Therapy,* vol. 23, pp. 52-60; as quoted in "Families Are Talking—Adolescents Would Prefer Parents as Primary Sexuality Educators," SIECUS Report Supplement, http://one.center-school.org/search-document-detail.php?ID=642.

7. "Talking to Your Teen About Sexuality," Hillsborough County University of Florida Extension, http://hillsboroughfcs.ifas.ufl.edu/FamilyPubsA-Z/sexuality.pdf.

8. Linda Klepacki, "Dear Parents: Let's Talk About Doing," PureInti macy.org, www.pureintimacy.org/piArticles/A000000584.cfm, citing a 2004 Focus on the Family article.

9. Mark and Grace Driscoll, "How To Talk To Your Kids About Sex," Resurgence, accessed February 15, 2012, http://theresurgence.com/2011/02/28/how-to-talk-to-your-kids-about-sex.

Chapter 7—Who Do Kids Want to Learn About Sex From?

1. "How to Talk to Your Kids About Anything," Talking With Kids About Tough Issues—a national campaign by Children Now and the Kaiser Family Foundation, http://www.talkwithkids.org/first.html.

2. B. Albert, "With One Voice 2004: America's Adults and Teens Sound Off About Teen Pregnancy," (Washington, DC: National Campaign to Prevent Teen Pregnancy, 2004); as quoted in Barbara Dafoe Whitehead and Marline Pearson, "Making a Love Connection," The National Campaign to Prevent Teen and Unplanned Pregnancy," thenationalcampaign.org.

3. Hutchinson and Cooney, 1998; Kreinin et al., 2001; Somers and Surmann, 2004; as quoted in Robert Crooks and Karla Baur, "Initiating Conversations When Children Do Not Ask Questions," The Talk Institute, www.thetalkinstitute.com/articles/initiating.html.

4. Kay S. Hymowitz, "It's Morning After in America," *City Journal,* spring 2004, www.manhattan-institute.org/cfml/printable.cfm?id=1337.

5. "Birds and Bees: Tips for Having 'The Talk' With Kids," ABC News (*Good Morning America*, September 22, 2011), http://abcnews.go.com/blogs/health/2011/09/22/birds-and-bees-tips-for-having-the-talk-with-kids-2/.

Chapter 8—Why Do I Need to Talk to My Kids About Sex?

1. Kristin Zolten, MA, and Nicholas Long, PhD, "Talking to Children About Sex," Center for Effective Parenting, 1997, www.parenting-ed.org/hand outs/sex.pdf.

2. Robert Crooks and Karla Baur, "Initiating Conversations When Children Do Not Ask Questions," The Talk Institute, www.thetalkinstitute.com/arti cles/initiating.html.

3. Maggi Ruth P. Boyer, "What to Do When They Just Won't Talk!" Advocates for Youth, www.advocatesforyouth.org/parents/164?task=view.

Chapter 9—Doesn't Talking About It Encourage It?

1. "Myths About Sexuality Education," Sexuality Education Resource Center Manitoba, Inc., rev. 2010, www.serc.mb.ca/content/dload/MythsAbout SexualityEducation%20/file.

2. Cheryl B. Aspy et al., *Journal of Adolescence* 30 (2007): pp. 449-466; as quoted in "Parental Involvement and Children's Well-Being," FamilyFacts. org, www.familyfacts.org/briefs/40/parental-involve ment-and-childrens-well-being.

3. Karin Suesser, PhD, and Matthew Doll, PhD, "Beyond the Birds and the Bees: How To Talk With Children About Sexuality," www .drsuesser.com/articles/talking_about_sex.pdf.

4. "Silence Breeds Babies," Campaign For Our Children, Inc., 2008, www. cfoc.org/index.php/parent-resource-center/talking-with-your-kids-about-sex/.

Chapter 10—When Is the "Age-Appropriate" Time to Talk About Sex?

1. Jen Boyer, "Talking to Kids About Sex," Balanced Living, www.balanced mag.com/2011/06/talking-to-kids-about-sex.

2. Alice Park, "Parents' Sex Talk with Kids: Too Little, Too Late," *Time*/CNN, Dec. 2007, 2009; www.time.com/time/health/article/0,8599,1945759,00 .html; emphasis (italics) added by authors.

3. Boyer.

4. Sue Simonson, "The Forgotten Years: Ones that may well be the key to Teen Pregnancy Prevention," Without Regret, accessed February 14, 2012, www.without-regret.org/tier2/articles.html.

5. "Broaching the Birds and the Bees," WebMD, November 26, 2001, www .webmd.com/sex-relationships/features/broaching-birds-bees.

6. Adapted from "How to Talk to Your Kids about Sex," Keeping Kids Healthy, accessed 2012, www.montekids.org/kkh/topics/how-to-talk-to-your-kids-about-sex/.

7. Dr. Corey Allan, "How To Talk To Your Children About Sex," Simple Mom, June 14, 2010, http://simplemom.net/how-to-talk-to-your-children-about-sex/.

Chapter 11—Do I Start with the "Big Talk"?

1. M. Raffaelli, K. Bogenschneider, and M.F. Flood, "Parent-teen Communication about Sexual Topics," *Journal of Family Issues*, vol. 19, pp. 315-333.

2. Deb Koster, "Talking to Kids About Sex," Family Fire, April 13, 2007, family fire.com/parenting/articles/Talking-to-Kids-About-Sex.

3. "Talking with Kids: A Parent's Guide to Sex Education," National PTA, Chicago, IL, 2002, p. 9, accessed at http://eric.ed.gov/PDFS/ED470698.pdf.

4. "How to talk to your child about sex," Psychologies, website accessed Feb. 2, 2012, www.psychologies.co.uk/family/how-to-talk-to-your-child-about-sex/.

Chapter 12—What Can Happen If I Don't Talk to My Kids About Sex?

1. Jack Wellman, "How to Talk to Your Children about Sex? A Christian Perspective," What Christians Want to Know, July 14, 2011, www.whatchristianswanttoknow.com/how-to-talk-to-your-children-about-sex-a-christian-perspective/.

2. Jill Manning, "Why the Government Should Care about Pornography," testimony before U.S. Senate Committee on the Judiciary, Nov. 10, 2005. Web 9, Nov. 2005, www.heritage.org/Research/Testimony/Pornographys-Impact-on-Marriage-amp-The-Family.

Chapter 13—What If My Kids Are Too Curious About Sex?

1. National Physicians Center for Family Resources, "Sex Talk Starters," Pure intimacy.org, www.pureintimacy.org/piArticles/A000000596.cfm.

2. Clea McNeely, MA, DrPH, and Jayne Blanchard, "The Teen Years Explained: A Guide to Healthy Adolescent Development," Center for Adolescent Health at Johns Hopkins Bloomberg School of Public Health, 2009.

3. McNeely and Blanchard.

4. Margaret Renkl, "The Birds and the Bees and Curious Kids," Parenting.com, accessed Feb. 14, 2012, www.parenting.com/article/kids-and-sexuality.

Chapter 15—How Much Knowledge Must I Have?

1. Clea McNeely, MA, DrPH, and Jayne Blanchard, "The Teen Years Explained: A Guide to Healthy Adolescent Development," Center for Adolescent Health at Johns Hopkins Bloomberg School of Public Health, 2009.

2. Keith Ferrell, "Adolescent Sexuality: Talk the Talk Before They Walk the Walk," Healthy Children Magazine, winter 2008, www.healthychildren.org/English/ages-stages/teen/dating-sex/pages/Adolescent-Sexuality-Talk-the-Talk-Before-They-Walk-the-Walk.aspx?nfstatus=401&nftoken=00000000-0000-0000-0000-000000000000&nfstatusdescription=ERROR%3a+No+local+token.

3. Kristin Zolten, MA, and Nicholas Long, PhD, "Talking to Children About Sex," Center for Effective Parenting, 1997, www.parenting-ed.org/handouts/sex.pdf.

Chapter 16—Shouldn't Certain Issues Be Off-Limits?

1. Jerald Newberry, "When Kids Ask Tough Questions About Sex," Advocates for Youth, 2008, www.advocatesforyouth.org/parents/176?task=view.

2. Kristin Zolten, MA, and Nicholas Long, PhD, "Talking to Children About Sex," Center for Effective Parenting, 1997, www.parenting-ed.org/hand outs/sex.pdf.

3. Jack Wellman, "How to Talk To Your Children about Sex? A Christian Perspective," What Christians Want to Know, July 14, 2011, www .whatchristianswanttoknow.com/how-to-talk-to-your-children-about-sex-a-christian-perspective/.

Chapter 17—How Often Should I Talk to My Kids About Sex?

1. "How to Talk to Your Kids About Anything," Talking With Kids About Tough Issues—a national campaign by Children Now and the Kaiser Family Foundation, www.talkwithkids.org/first.html.

2. Margaret Renkl, "The Birds and the Bees and Curious Kids," Parenting.com, accessed Feb. 14, 2012, www.parenting.com/article/kids-and-sexuality.

3. Steven C. Martino, PhD, Marc N. Elliott, PhD, et al., "Beyond the 'Big Talk': The Roles of Breadth and Repetition in Parent-Adolescent Communication About Sexual Topics," *Pediatrics*, 2008, http://pediatrics.aappublica tions.org/content/121/3/e612.full.html.

Chapter 18—Won't They Think I'm Obsessed If I Keep Harping on the Sex Issue?

1. "Families are Talking—Teens Talk About TV, Sex, and Real Life," SIECUS Report Supplement, http://one.center-school.org/search-document-detail. php?ID=827.

2. Linda Klepacki, "What Your Teens Need to Know About Sex," Focus on the Family, 2005, www.focusonthefamily.com/lifechallenges/love_and_sex/ purity/what_your_teens_need_to_know_about_sex.aspx.

3. Adapted from "Teachable Moments," the "Wait for Sex" parent workshop curriculum, ReCAPP—ETR Associates' Resource Center for Adolescent Pregnancy Prevention, 2004, www.etr.org/recapp/documents/freebies/ teachablemoments.pdf.

4. Task Force on the Sexualization of Girls, "Report of the APA Task Force on the Sexualization of Girls," American Psychological Association, 2010; www.apa.org/pi/women/programs/girls/report-full.pdf.

5. Adapted from "Families are Talking—Teens Talk About TV, Sex, and Real Life," SIECUS Report Supplement, http://one.center-school.org/search-document-detail.php?ID=827.

6. Wendy L. Sellers, "Talking to Your Child about Relationships and Sexuality," EduGuide, accessed February 15, 2012, www.eduguide.org/library/viewarticle/339.

7. "Talking to Your Teen About Sexuality," Hillsborough County University of Florida Extension, http://hillsboroughfcs.ifas.ufl.edu/FamilyPubsA-Z/sexuality.pdf.

8. "Talking to Your Teen."

9. "Talking to Your Teen."

10. "Talking to Your Teen."

11. "Talking to Your Teen."

12. "Talking to Your Teen."

13. Esther J. Cepeda, "Talking to Kids About Sex: Conversations Worth Having," *Seattle Times*, October 9, 2011, http://seattletimes.nwsource.com/html/opinion/2016439742_cepada10.html.

14. Deb Roffman, "Talking to Your Kids About Sex: Deborah Roffman Offers Parents Advice," Make it Better, www.makeitbetter.net/family/parenting/939-talking-to-your-kids-about-sex-deborah-roffman-offers-parents-advice.

Chapter 19—Just How Much Should I Monitor My Kids' World?

1. Thanks to Joshua DeVries for providing this section.

Chapter 20—When Does Monitoring Become an Invasion of Privacy?

1. Mary VanClay, "How to talk to your child about sex," BabyCenter LLC., accessed Feb. 15, 2012 http://cdrcp.com/pdf/How%20to%20talk%20to%20your%20child%20about%20sex.pdf.

Chapter 21—How Do I Respond to My Kids' "First Love"?

1. "Talking to Your Teen About Sexuality," Hillsborough County University of Florida Extension, http://hillsboroughfcs.ifas.ufl.edu/FamilyPubsA-Z/sexuality.pdf.

2. Clea McNeely, MA, DrPH, and Jayne Blanchard, "The Teen Years Explained: A Guide to Healthy Adolescent Development," Center for Adolescent Health at Johns Hopkins Bloomberg School of Public Health, 2009.

3. "Talking Back," The National Campaign to Prevent Teen and Unplanned Pregnancy, 2012, www.thenationalcampaign.org/parents/talking_back.aspx.

Chapter 22—What Sexual Rules or Boundaries Do I Set for My Child?

1. "Talking Back," The National Campaign to Prevent Teen and Unplanned Pregnancy, 2012, www.thenationalcampaign.org/parents/talking_back .aspx.

2. "Ten Tips for Parents: To Help Their Children Avoid Teen Pregnancy," The National Campaign to Prevent Teen and Unplanned Pregnancy, accessed Feb. 6, 2012, www.thenationalcampaign.org/resources/toTips.aspx.

3. Glenn T. Stanton, "The Most Effective Deterrent," PureIntimacy .org, accessed Feb. 16, 2012, http://www.pureintimacy.org/piArticles/ A000000608.cfm.

4. Eileen M. Hart, "Teens, Sex and Media," 2002, accessed Feb. 13, 2012, http://www.frankwbaker.com/MediaLitEd.pdf.

5. "Pornography Statistics," Covenant Eyes, www.covenanteyes. com/2010/01/06/updated-pornography-statistics/.

6. "Youth Risk Behavior Surveillance—United States, 1995, Surveillance Summaries," *Morbidity and Mortality Weekly,* September 27, 1996.

7. "The Truth About Adolescent Sexuality," Education.com, quoting the Sexuality Information and Education Council of the United States, 2005, www .education.com/reference/article/Ref_Truth_About/.

8. "How Can I Lovingly Snoop On My Teen?" Harvest USA, 2007, www. harvestusa.org/index.php?option=com_content&view=article&id=1 72%3Ahow-can-i-lovingly-snoop-on-my-teen&catid=15%3Acontact us&Itemid=1.

9. "How Can I Lovingly Snoop On My Teen?"

10. "How Can I Lovingly Snoop On My Teen?"

11. "Teaching Children About Healthy Sexuality," Health and Fitness, May 2, 2011, http://www.kylegabouer.com/teaching-children-about-healthy-sex uality.html.

Chapter 23—How Realistic Is It to Expect Them to Wait?

1. Adapted from Lakita Garth, *The Naked Truth: About Sex, Love and Relationships* (Ventura, CA: Gospel Light, 2007), p. 135.

Chapter 24—How Do I Get My Kids to Treat the Opposite Sex Properly?

1. Dr. Corey Allan, "How to Talk to Your Children About Sex," Simple Mom, June 14, 2010, http://simplemom.net/how-to-talk-to-your-children-about-sex.

Chapter 25—What About "Sexting," and What Can I Do About It?

1. Al Menconi, "Responsible Text Messaging Tips," August 18, 2011, http://almenconi.blogspot.com/2011/08/responsible-text-messaging-tips.html.

2. Menconi.

3. Menconi.

4. As quoted in Sharon Jayson, "Parents, talk about sex, even if teens tune you out," *USA Today*, Oct. 13, 2011, www.usatoday.com/news/health/wellness/teen-ya/story/2011-10-12/Experts-Talk-sex-with-your-teen-even-if-they-tune-you-out/50745740/1.

Chapter 26—How Do I Help My Kids Resist Sexual Pressure?

1. "Helping Teens Resist Sexual Pressure," HealthyChildren.org, quoting American Academy of Pediatrics, "Caring for Your Teenager," accessed February 14, 2012, www.healthychildren.org/English/ages-stages/teen/dating-sex/pages/Helping-Teens-Resist-Sexual-Pressure.aspx.

2. "Parenting—Talking to Your Teen about Sex and Oral Sex," Dr. Phil.com, accessed Feb. 15, 2012, www.drphil.com/articles/article/51.

Chapter 28—Most Kids Don't Believe Oral Sex Is Having Sex. How Do I Correct Their Misperception?

1. Jim Liebelt, "Culture Snapshot of Adolescent Sex and Sexuality," January 29, 2007, HomeWord Center for Youth and Family, www.homeword.com/culture-snapshot-adolescent-sexuality-ta-a-1161.html.

2. Liebelt.

3. 2003 series of national surveys conducted for the Kaiser Family Foundation (KFF) and *Seventeen* magazine.

4. B.L. Halpern-Felsher et al., "Oral versus vaginal sex among adolescents: Perceptions, attitudes, and behavior," *Pediatrics*, 2005 (vol. 115, no. 4), pp. 845-851. Debby Golonka, "Talking with children about sex," Revolution Health, April 22, 2008, www.revolutionhealth.com/healthy-living/parenting/talking-with-children-about-sex.

5. Chris Wagner, "Oral Sex is Sex, and Most Teens Don't Know it," Center for Parent/Youth Understanding, www.cpyu.org/pageview_p.asp?pageID=18565.

6. Wagner.

7. Wagner.

8. Wagner.

9. Wagner.

10. Wagner.

11. "Parenting—Talking to Your Teen about Sex and Oral Sex," Dr. Phil.com, accessed Feb. 15, 2012, www.drphil.com/articles/article/51.

12. Roxanne Khamsi, "Oral sex can cause throat cancer," *NewScientist,* May 9, 2007, www.newscientist.com/article/dn11819-oral-sex-can-cause-throat-cancer.html.

13. Julie Sharp, "Oral Sex Linked to Throat Cancer: A virus contracted through oral sex is the cause of some throat cancers, say US scientists," BBC News, May 10, 2007, http://news.bbc.co.uk/2/hi/health/6639461.stm.

14. Sharp.

Chapter 29—How Does a Healthy Self-Image Protect My Child from Premarital Sex?

1. Rob Jackson, "Teaching Children Healthy Sexuality," Focus on the Family, 2004, www.focusonthefamily.com/parenting/sexuality/teaching_children_healthy_sexuality.aspx.

2. The National Campaign to Prevent Teen Pregnancy, *Rethinking Responsibility: Reflections on Sex and Sexuality* (Washington, DC: The National Campaign to Prevent Teen Pregnancy, 2009).

3. Laura Flynn McCarthy, "Pregnancy Test," *Family Circle,* February 2011, www.familycircle.com.

4. "Talking With Kids About HIV and AIDS," Talk With Your Kids, www.talkwithyourkids.org/aids.html.

Chapter 30—Six Ways to Become Wise Parents Who Talk to Their Kids About Sex

1. "The Truth About Adolescent Sexuality," SIECUS—the Sexuality Information and Education Council of the United States, www.siecus.org/pubs/fact/fact0020.html.

2. Glenn T. Stanton, "The Most Effective Deterrent," PureIntimacy.org, accessed Feb. 16, 2012, www.pureintimacy.org/piArticles/A000000608.cfm.

3. The National Campaign to Prevent Teen and Unplanned Pregnancy, "Bridging the Divide: Involving the Faith Community in Teen Pregnancy

Prevention," October 10, 2007, www.thenational
campaign.org/resources/pdf/Bridging_FINAL.pdf.

4. Laura Flynn McCarthy, "Pregnancy Test," *Family Circle*, February 2011,
   www.familycircle.com.

5. The National Campaign to Prevent Teen Pregnancy, *Rethinking Responsibility: Reflections on Sex and Sexuality* (Washington, DC: The National
   Campaign to Prevent Teen Pregnancy, 2009).

6. R. Lerner, "Can Abstinence Work?: An Analysis of the Best Friends Program," *Adolescent & Family Health*, 2005 (vol. 3, no. 4), pp. 185-192; as
   quoted in The National Campaign to Prevent Teen Pregnancy, *Rethinking Responsibility: Reflections on Sex and Sexuality* (Washington, DC: The
   National Campaign to Prevent Teen Pregnancy, 2009).

Other Resources from Josh McDowell

The Bare Facts book and DVD resources

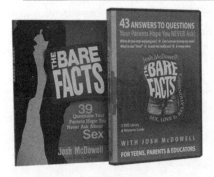

The Bare Facts: The Truth about Sex, Love & Relationships delivers frank and intimate answers to the top questions students ask about sex, love, and relationships. Josh believes no question is off limits and that knowledge, not ignorance, is the key to youthful purity. Using relevant statistics, entertaining anecdotes, real stories, and biblical insight, *The Bare Facts* book and DVD will equip young people with the facts they are sorely missing.

The Father Connection

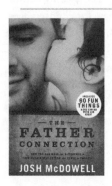

Updated and redesigned for a new generation of dads, *The Father Connection* looks at ten parenting qualities inspired by the ultimate model of fatherhood. A dad who embraces these godly characteristics will make all the difference in a child, boosting their self-esteem and sense of purpose and helping him or her to feel loved and secure. Each chapter focuses on a different godly characteristic and suggests ways for you to become the kind of influence you have always wanted to be in your children's lives. Includes 60 fun things a dad can do with his kids.

How to Be a Hero to Your Kids

You don't have to be a super-parent to be a hero to your kids. All it takes is love, motivation, and a workable plan. Josh McDowell and Dick Day offer a six-point, biblically-based plan for positive parenting that will set you on the path to being a hero to your child.

The Amazing Bible Adventure for Kids
Finding the Awesome Truth in God's Word

Josh McDowell and Kevin Johnson

Josh McDowell, author of *The Unshakable Truth*® and many others, joins pastor and bestselling author Kevin Johnson to map out a quest for children ages 7 to 11—a quest that will lead them to the discovery that God is truth, and that real happiness comes from knowing him as he is revealed in his Word. With fun facts, questions, and laugh-out-loud stories, McDowell and Johnson simplify the tough concepts and bring boys and girls to the most amazing treasure of all!

The Awesome Book of Bible Answers for Kids

Josh McDowell and Kevin Johnson

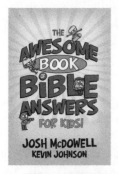

These concise, welcoming answers include key Bible verses and explorations of topics that matter most to kids ages 8 to 12: God's love; right and wrong; Jesus, the Holy Spirit, and God's Word; different beliefs and religions; church, prayer, and sharing faith. Josh and Kevin look at questions like...

• How do I know God wants to be my friend?

• Are parts of the Bible make-believe, or is everything true?

• Was Jesus a wimp?

• Why do some Christians not act like Christians?

• Can God make bad things turn out okay?

The next time a child in your life asks a good question, this practical and engaging volume will give you helpful tips and conversation ideas so you can connect with them and offer straight talk about faith in Jesus. *Includes an easy-to-use learning and conversation guide.*

Other Helpful Resources from Harvest House

Apologetics for a New Generation
A Biblical and Culturally Relevant Approach to Talking About God

Sean McDowell

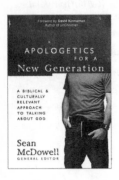

This generation's faith is constantly under attack from the secular media, skeptical teachers, and unbelieving peers. You may wonder, *How can I help?*

Working with young adults every day, Sean McDowell understands their situation and shares your concern. His first-rate team of contributors shows how you can help members of the new generation plant their feet firmly on the truth. Find out how you can walk them through the process of…

- formulating a biblical worldview and applying scriptural principles to everyday issues
- articulating their questions and addressing their doubts in a safe environment
- becoming confident in their faith and effective in their witness

The truth never gets old, but people need to hear it in fresh, new ways. Find out how you can effectively share the answers to life's big questions with a new generation.

150 Quick Questions to Get Your Kids Talking

Mary DeMuth

Do you ever wish your kids would open up and talk? Do you long to have meaningful and fun conversations as a family? Are you looking for creative ways to share God's grace with your kids and see how He is moving in their lives? This innovative resource is for you! It contains 150 quick, open-ended questions that are sure to prompt lively discussions that every member of the family will enjoy.

Some of these discussion starters are just for fun ("If you could be one zoo animal, what would you be?"), and others probe more deeply ("What has been the happiest day of your life so far?"). All of them are sure to get your kids talking and enrich your mealtime conversations.

52 Things Kids Need from a Dad
What Fathers Can Do to Make a Lifelong Difference

Jay Payleitner

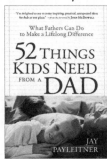

Good news—you are already the perfect dad for your kids! Still, you know you can grow. In these pages, Jay Payleitner, veteran radio producer and dad of five, offers a bounty of inspiring and unexpected insights:

- *straightforward rules:* "carry photos of your kids," "dad tucks in," and "kiss your wife in the kitchen"
- *candid advice that may be tough to hear:* "get right with your own dad," "throw out your porn," and "surrender control of the TV remote"
- *weird topics that at first seem absurd:* "buy Peeps," "spin a bucket over your head" and "rent a dolphin"

Surely, God—our heavenly Father—designed fatherhood to be a joy, a blessing, and a blast!

"I'm delighted to see so many inspiring, practical, unexpected ideas for dads in one place."

from the foreword by Josh McDowell

To learn more about Harvest House books and
to read sample chapters, log on to our website:

www.harvesthousepublishers.com

HARVEST HOUSE PUBLISHERS
EUGENE, OREGON